Walter Shephard Ufford

Fresh air Charity in the United States

Walter Shephard Ufford

Fresh air Charity in the United States

ISBN/EAN: 9783743333949

Manufactured in Europe, USA, Canada, Australia, Japa

Cover: Foto ©ninafisch / pixelio.de

Manufactured and distributed by brebook publishing software (www.brebook.com)

Walter Shephard Ufford

Fresh air Charity in the United States

FRESH AIR CHARITY

IN THE

UNITED STATES

BY

WALTER SHEPARD UFFORD, Ph.D.

RECENTLY FELLOW IN SOCIOLOGY IN COLUMBIA UNIVERSITY

CONTENTS.

CHAPTER I.
INTRODUCTORY.

	PAGE
The trend of events favorable to the charity	1
Problems arising from its rapid growth	2
Two Fresh Air conferences	3
The present inquiry suggested	4
Its scope as shown by the circular letter of inquiry	5
Sources of information and method of procedure	6
The limits of the inquiry; their justification	7
The summer philanthropies omitted	9

CHAPTER II.
STATISTICS OF FRESH AIR SOCIETIES OUTSIDE OF NEW YORK CITY.

Character and completeness of the data	10
Conditions thought to promote the charity	11
Location, names, and dates of the general societies	11
Summary of their distribution	12
Their nature	12
Rise and development of the charity	14
Its relation to similar movements abroad	19
Beneficiaries, significance and value of the term	20
Total expenditures.—an analysis	23
Statistics of beneficiaries and expenditures of 37 societies	26
Age classification	27
Statistics for 1895	28
Analysis and discussion	30
Sex	31
Two types of the work—day excursions and country week	32
Cost, per capita, 1895, (and note on "state-help")	35
Form of entertainment	39

CHAPTER III.

FRESH AIR RELIEF IN NEW YORK CITY.

	PAGE
Conditions here especially favorable for the study	42
Three divisions of the subject	43

I. General Fresh Air Societies (descriptive).
- St. John's Guild ... 44
- Children's Aid Society ... 45
- Sanitarium for Hebrew Children ... 46
- Tribune Fresh Air Fund ... 48
- All Souls' Summer Home ... 52
- Bartholdi Crèche ... 54
- Life's Fresh Air Fund ... 55
- Association for Improving the Condition of the Poor ... 55
- George Junior Republic ... 57
- Little Mothers' Aid Association ... 60
- Summer Shelter of Morristown ... 60
- Gilbert A Robertson Home ... 61
- Laua ac Tela Society ... 62
- Christian Herald Children's Home ... 62

Statistics of these fourteen General Societies
- Table I.—General Statistics ... 63
- Analysis ... 64
- Table II.—Excursionists and Visitors in 1895 ... 66
- Analysis ... 67
- Adults and Children ... 67
- Table III.—Adults and Children in 1895 ... 68
- Ages of Child-Visitors ... 68
- Table IV.—Ages of Child-Visitors in 1895 ... 69
- Expenditures ... 69
- Cost of permanent equipment ... 70
- Table V.—Expenditures of the General Societies ... 71
- Analysis ... 72

II. New York's Parochial Agencies ... 73
- Limits observed in the tabulation ... 73
- Affiliations of the societies tabulated ... 74
- Denominational activity ... 74
- Remarks on Tables VI. and VII. ... 76
- Table VI.—Statistics of Parochial Societies for 1895 ... 77
- Table VII.—Expenditures of Parochial Societies for 1895 ... 78

III. Working Girl's Vacation Societies ... 78
- Their distinguishing characteristic ... 78
- New York Working Girls' Vacation Society ... 78
- Jewish Working Girls' Vacation Society ... 79
- The Vacation Farm Society ... 80
- Table VIII.—Statistics of Working Girls' Vacation Societies ... 80
- Analysis ... 81

Statistical summary of New York's Fresh Air work ... 83

CONTENTS.

CHAPTER IV.

DISCUSSION OF GENERAL PROBLEMS.

	PAGE
Topics treated	84
The various forms of Fresh Air relief	84
Day excursions	84
Country week	86
The family, and the "home" or colony	87
Methods employed in the selection of beneficiaries	90
Contributions of beneficiaries	91
English and American systems compared	92
Means taken to prevent duplication	93
Possibilities of such duplication in New York City	95
A hypothetical case	96
Opinions of workers	96
Objections to duplication	97
Statistics of a canvass of 200 families	98
Does the charity tend to pauperize its recipients	99
Self-operating checks	99
The charity as an educational force	100
Perfecting the philanthropy	102
Official opinions concerning its present needs	103
Its rewards	105
Conclusions	107
Bibliography	112

CHAPTER I.

INTRODUCTORY.

One of the latest and richest fruits of modern philanthropy is that embraced under the comprehensive title, Fresh Air Charity. Inspired, in some few instances, by similar movements abroad, its genesis has been in the main a product of local conditions and enthusiasms. The rapid development of our cities had sacrificed light and air to the pressing demands of modern industrialism. The tenement and the slum had come to be accepted as the price of material growth. Meanwhile attempts to mitigate rather than destroy the ills of congested populations were making. Dispensaries ministering freely to the sick, the growth of organized charity, the development of the college settlement, and the institutional church, are witnesses to a desire to alleviate the life of the poor at their own doors.

Contemporaneously with the massing of population in the cities has come, like the memory of a departed blessing, a hunger for the sea, the country and the mountains. The gospel of vacations and outdoor life has been proclaimed as the cure for the nervous exhaustion of urban conditions. Business, religion, education have adapted themselves to the demand for increased relaxation. Where time and money are boon companions it is an easy matter to take advantage of the leisure of the summer months. Happily those who regularly take themselves off to the country or the seashore have not been able entirely to forget the less fortunate denizens of the city who are left behind.

Another influence which has been at work in behalf of this philanthropy is the shifting of interest from the adult to the child. In religion, education, social reform, all questions of progress center about the child. The child is recognized as the salvable element in society. The kindergarten, the manual training school, young people's religious societies, the innumerable clubs for boys and for girls, all confirm what is a matter of common observation. The child is set in the midst to-day after the example of two thousand years ago.

This growing respect for the sacredness of childhood, coupled with the economic and social conditions already referred to, has made Fresh Air relief, as it exists at present, both spontaneous and inevitable. Scarcely any appeals, except in behalf of those actually perishing, find so general and hearty response as do those for fresh air for the babies and children.

The philanthropy is largely the product of our own generation. Some of the pioneers of the movement are still in their prime. They have lived to see their early efforts generously sustained and widely imitated. To-day in New York City alone, twenty-nine churches of one denomination unite in this work. Fourteen general and nonsectarian agencies, and no fewer than nineteen denominational enterprises or special societies conducting Fresh Air Homes, are in the field, to say nothing of the innumerable allied or private instrumentalities.

It is not surprising that the friends of organized charity, especially in a city like New York, should look upon this rapid and uncoordinated multiplication of Fresh Air societies with some misgiving. Absence of mutual conference or systematic coöperation among the workers has long been regarded as a misfortune, although not a few promoters of the expanding charity have maintained in theory and practice that there could be no such thing as too much fresh air for anybody. The question at once arises whether there is something in the nature of this particular form of relief which makes it an exception to the general principles of scientific charity. Can Fresh Air societies, for example, afford to act except upon knowledge gained by thorough investigation? Ought they to endeavor impartially to provide for all who are worthily in need of their beneficence? To this end ought they to use means to prevent unwise duplication and the bestowal of relief upon those who might provide for their own outing? Should parents be encouraged to contribute something, no matter how small, to the expense of the holiday? Need we have any fear that the charity will ever make paupers of the children who receive it?

These questions cannot be answered without a study of the methods actually employed in Fresh Air relief and their results. Up to this time no such inquiry as the present one has been attempted. Each agency at work in the field has presented its own case to the public, usually to find a cordial endorsement shown by enlarged contributions. It is scarcely too much to affirm that the philanthropy has been regarded as a kind of summer recreation in which the rules that obtain during the more serious portions of the year might safely be suspended. Now and then a vigorous protest has been entered against making the charity the one exception to the general principle that it is always dangerous to give something for nothing. All warnings of this sort have been quickly forgotten in the enthusiasm of the moment.

Two conferences on "Fresh Air Work" have been held in New York City under the auspices of the Charity Organization Society. A printed report of the first of these gatherings of workers called together in 1888 thus outlines the general situation: "Rapid growth brings to light hidden difficulties. The removal of difficulties requires investigation and the application of wise methods. Such is the history of Fresh Air work in New York City. The multitude of children who have been sent out into the country in recent years, the varying obstacles encountered, and the diverging plans of treatment, have made a comparison of methods more necessary than ever. It was the recognition of this fact that led to the calling of a conference of Fresh Air workers by certain of those interested in that noble charity." The committee in charge of the arrangements had suggested these topics for consideration: "Invited Guests, Boarding Out, and Colonization;" "Medical Examination and Cleanliness;" "Partial Payments by Parents, including carfares;" "Selection and Classification;" "Instruction;" "Food;" "Should Children be Expected to Work;" "Repeaters." Concerning the last topic the report says: "The discussion on this point was full and interesting. All present felt the need of stopping so evil a custom—a custom which robbed one child of pleasure and profit for the undue gratification of another. Mrs. Wolcott, an agent of the Charity Organization Society, related how, when three out of five missionaries in her district complied with the request for coöperation, there was discovered in the lists compared thirty per cent. of duplication. . . . It was suggested by Mr. Kellogg that the Charity Organization Society were able and willing to make up a central register of the names sent by the various agents."

Resolutions, expressing the sense of the meeting on each of the topics under consideration, were passed. With regard to duplication it was resolved: "That the Charity Organization Society offers an efficient agency for the prevention of repeating. That a conference of missionaries and other Fresh Air workers should be held early in the season, at some central place in each part of the city, for a comparison of the lists of children (the offices of the respective District Committees of the Charity Organization Society are freely offered for such conferences), and that cordial coöperation is the only power that can put down the evils of repeating." Three years elapsed during which no action seems to have been taken to put into practice the suggestions of the conference. A second gathering was called together in 1891. As a result of its deliberations a circular letter was addressed to the societies and churches engaged in the work. This letter invited them "to furnish to the Charity Organization Society lists of the names and addresses of their beneficiaries *who had received a week or more vacation during the summer,* so that such lists may be compared at the end of the season in order to discover what duplications, if any, have occurred." This, however, was not the sole purpose of the communication. The letter continued: "It is also desired to elicit such information concerning difficulties that arise and obstacles that are encountered during the summer, in the experience of all, so that at the close of the summer a comparison may be made and remedies and improvements devised. It was felt that such information was necessary in order to ascertain the magnitude of real or supposed abuses and to deal with them intelligently."

This request for a list of the beneficiaries of each society and also for such experiences and suggestions as might be deemed helpful was, like the recommendations of the conference of 1888, practically unheeded. Unity of action on the part of Fresh Air societies seems to-day as far off as ever. Meanwhile the work has continued to grow both in variety and volume. To what proportions it has actually attained, not only in New York City, but in the country at large, the following statistical study will serve to indicate.

Notwithstanding the apparent failure of the two conferences held at the instance of the Charity Organization Society, the conclusions there reached have not been entirely forgotten. The feeling expressed at the conference of 1891, "that the danger line had been reached in this department of charity," is still prevalent among experienced Fresh Air workers of the city. William Howe Tolman, Ph. D., the general agent of the New York Association for Improving the Condition of the Poor, first directed the writer's attention to the field covered by the present inquiry. The coöperation of the Association was freely offered by Dr. Tolman in the interest of a thorough statistical investigation. A list of questions was prepared, and circulated in the name of the N. Y. A. I. C. P. The report of the society for 1895 thus speaks with reference to this inquiry: "The great danger in Fresh Air work is the tendency to pauperization. The boy or girl receives a day's outing free, then the child will want a week at the Seaside Home, or the parents will think that the society should help them during the winter. When Fresh Air work is not planned with the greatest wisdom, and careful selection made of those to come within the scope, there is danger that more harm than good will result. To ascertain the salient features of the Fresh Air work of the various societies and churches, the following inquiries are being sent:

1. Does your Society undertake the Summer Charity, commonly known as the Fresh Air Work?
2. What other societies or churches in your city are also engaged in this work?
3. In what year was your work inaugurated?
4. Total number of beneficiaries to date?
5. Expenditures (excluding construction expenses) to date?
6. Number of men, women, children, sent in 1895?
7. Number sent for week(s)? Number sent for day(s)?
8. Total expenditures, 1895?
9. Are beneficiaries sent to private families or to your own homes?
10. How are the children selected; by your own visitor ; through other societies ; or otherwise?
11. Do parents, children or friends share the expense of each outing for the day or week?
12. What proportion?
13. Are any means employed to prevent duplication by churches and societies engaged in this work? If so, what?
14. Is there any tendency on the part of the recipients to come upon the Society for assistance in other directions, apparently as a result of this work?
15. Is any kind of instruction attempted at your Summer Homes?
16. If so, of what nature?
17. From your experience, will you give any suggestions as to a better and more thorough organization of this work?
18. How can the work be improved?
     (a)   (b)   (c)
19. Does it pay?"

There are in the United States no fewer than 129 relief societies which have adopted wholly or in part Charity Organization principles, and which are in correspondence with one another as occasion demands. These societies represent communities whose population aggregated, at the last census, 11,450,000. In December, 1895, the above letter was sent to each of these 129 societies and also to churches and other organizations in New York City engaged in this work. Of the 128 relief societies outside of New York City addressed in this way, 48 replied to the circular letter; 25 of these answered that no Fresh Air work was attempted in their respective cities or towns, while 23 replied in the affirmative and furnished information more or less complete. In several instances the original letter had been referred for answer to the particular society in the town undertaking the work. In other cases the name of such society or societies was furnished by way of answer to the second question of the circular. In the latter instance, a letter was forwarded at once directly to the society mentioned.

After waiting several months for further replies, another attempt was made after this fashion. The Charity Organization Societies in all the cities of 100,000 inhabitants or over, not already heard from, were addressed, this time with a personal letter to the secretary of the society. Any other agencies known to be doing Fresh Air work, but from whom no direct information had as yet been obtained, were similarly approached. Not infrequently, a correspondence protracted through the summer of 1896 was necessary before the facts desired could be secured. The tables are themselves witnesses to not a few failures to make the returns complete. In New York City, the inquiry was simplified by easy access to the agencies themselves. Reliance upon correspondence was, if possible, less satisfactory here than elsewhere. Personal visits, explaining the purpose of the inquiry, proved the one effective way of ensuring the coöperation of the societies and churches concerned.

In the case of the latter, it was seen very early in the course of the inquiry that it would be too much to expect from them a summary of their Fresh Air work, beyond the current year. Seldom were complete files of their annual reports or year books available, nor is it the custom with such religious societies to carry forward from year to year the totals of their Fresh Air work. The matter was much simpler in the case of the non-sectarian societies. Accustomed to render an account of their stewardship to the general public, it was only a matter of time to secure the data sought. It but remains to justify the classification adopted in the compilation of the results, before proceeding to the presentation of the statistical material.

In any study of Fresh Air charity in the United States it would manifestly be impracticable to attempt to include the work of all the parochial[1] agencies interested in the philanthropy. Some idea of the possibilities of their activity may be had by reference to the statistics of New York City. The secretary of the "Country Week," of Boston, after mentioning more than thirty agencies engaged in Fresh Air charity in that city, concludes the catalogue, as if in despair of doing everybody justice, by saying: "and nearly every other church and society in Boston." There are at least two reasons for omitting these parochial societies, besides the evident impossibility of furnishing anything like a complete list of them. In the first place, where systematic records are kept—which is by no means always the case, such records are frequently regarded as the private concern of the particular church or society. The statistician is not unlikely to be looked upon as a newsmonger and his request for the transcription of statistical data, as a bit of unwarranted intrusion. The second reason is the desire to avoid duplication in the statistics, for the omission referred to is often more apparent than real. Of the various organizations in Boston reported as doing Fresh Air work, nearly all were, in a greater or less degree, coöperating with "Country Week." To prevent duplication of records, it is necessary to count the beneficiary, not in his own home, nor in the hands of the mission or agency that vouches for his worthiness and need, but as the ward of the society that actually transports him to the country and is responsible for his entertainment. An illustration of this principle is furnished by the Baptist Young People's Union of New York. In 1895, twenty-nine Baptist agencies sent children to the country under the auspices of the Union. Each of these twenty-nine religious societies might truly report themselves as engaged in Fresh Air work. An enumeration of their beneficiaries, together with those of the Union, would have led to an inflation of 100 per cent. There is much also that rightly enough falls under the head of Fresh Air charity which is not of informing value in an inquiry like the present one. There are, for instance, the single day's outings occasionally provided in certain towns and cities for the poor of the community.

---

[1] By a *parochial* society is meant one which ministers to its own membership or constituency. Social settlements as well as churches would be included in the term.

Often, as one of our correspondents has expressed it with regard to her own city:[1] "The work in this line is not so much from the necessity of giving the beneficiaries fresher and purer air as to bring a little brightness and diversion into their lives." Outings of this kind, although of the nature of picnics, are not on this account to be despised, especially when properly safeguarded so that the physically and materially destitute are the ones actually reached.[2] Naturally, however, a study like the present one, pursued for the purpose of throwing light upon the problems attaching to Fresh Air relief, interests itself primarily in the more serious and constant efforts systematically to reach the poor and destitute sick of our cities and towns. It is therefore to the general and regular types of the philanthropy as distinguished either from the parochial, on the one hand, and the occasional, on the other, that this immediate portion of the inquiry addresses itself. When we confine our attention to a single city, like New York, it becomes practicable to present statistics for both general Fresh Air charities and those more or less limited in their field of operation.

Even in that case, great care is necessary to avoid duplication of records, while the impossibility of securing from the churches statistics of their work for a succession of years, has forbidden a comprehensive tabulation of the Fresh Air activity of these agencies.

There are two forms of this philanthropy, frequently included under the broad title, "Fresh Air Work," that do not properly belong to an inquiry like the present. Many institutions, such as hospitals and orphanages, maintain summer homes to which they transfer during the heated term their inmates or convalescents. With these we have nothing to do. They are branches of permanent and continuous charities and are not called upon to face the problems with which the present investigation concerns itself. There is, in the second place, a large amount of Fresh Air work which does not fall under the head of relief-giving. None the less is it nobly philanthropic. We refer to those efforts, whose name is legion, to provide boarding places at low rates for gentlewomen and working people. The numerous summer homes of the Young Women's Christian Association, of the Girls' Friendly Societies, of the Vacation Rest Societies, the Retreats for Nurses, and other

---

[1] Bangor, Me.

[2] The following cities report general excursions for a single day in 1895: Louisville, Ky.; New Brunswick and Trenton, N. J.; Brockton, Mass. Doubtless there were many others not reported.

similar institutions are the fruit of this kind of philanthropy. Permanent quarters are provided by generously disposed individuals or societies. Board and rooms are to be had at a nominal price. The guests are not allowed to consider themselves objects of charity but every means is taken to maintain their self-respect. Several homes coming under one or the other of these heads have been brought to our attention but are excluded by the classification adopted.

In our study then, of Fresh Air Charity, these four types of endeavor will be neglected:—

1. Parochial Fresh Air Charities, or those intended to meet the needs of a particular society or parish.[1]

2. "Free Excursions," given but once in the course of the season and not always on successive years.

3. Branch Hospitals for Convalescents, Summer Orphanages and the like.

4. Summer Homes where the principle of "self-help" predominates.[2]

---

[1] These are included in the study of Fresh Air societies in New York City.

[2] A correspondent thus describes one of these Holiday Houses of the Girls' Friendly Society: "The board is $3.00 per week and that covers the expense of the table and the wages of four women servants. We raise enough money to give the girls drives and to cover the expense of keeping the place in order and certain other incidentals. Every girl who comes pays her own board and her railroad fare, which is $1.55 for the round trip. Of course, in many instances, this money has been furnished either by the Sick Relief Fund of her branch or by individual persons, but we have no means of knowing about this, as it is not our affair."

CHAPTER II.

STATISTICS OF FRESH AIR SOCIETIES.

The method employed in collecting the statistical material for a study of Fresh Air relief, as well as the limitations imposed by the nature of the inquiry have already been set forth. We are now prepared to consider, at some length, the data obtained in answer to the questions addressed to all the General Fresh Air Societies known to exist in the United States. In a few minor instances only—some half dozen in all—have returns eventually been wanting. The results, therefore, as tabulated may be looked upon with considerable confidence as embodying the work of the great majority of these agencies throughout the country.

Of the 61 places replying to the circular letter, 35 report that Fresh Air work is being prosecuted in their respective cities or towns. The replies furnished by 11 of these, however, show that the work described does not fall within the scope of the present study. 26 places answer in the negative. The presumption is in favor of supposing that of the nearly 70 cities or towns sending no replies, the large majority had no work of the kind to report. This conclusion is based upon the facts: (1) That a society doing general Fresh Air work, or knowing of its being done within its own town, might be expected to feel sufficient local pride to publish the matter abroad; (2) that a majority of the places heard from, either replied in the negative, or reported work outside the field of investigation; (3) from the character of the towns not heard from, their situation, size or material resources.

Of the 28 cities of over 100,000 inhabitants at the last census,

- 17 are known to sustain General Fresh Air Charities and these appear in the statistical tables.
- 4 report charities outside the present field.
- 4 answer in the negative.
- 3 have not been heard from, but in only one of these is it probable that the work is carried on.

Among the 26 places reporting: "No Fresh Air Work," are many of the smaller Eastern cities and several of the larger cities of the West, like Denver, Kansas City, Portland, Ore., Seattle and San Francisco.

Many of the answers throw light upon the conditions that are supposed to favor the growth of the charity. The secretary of the Charity Organization Society of Denver, writes: "The superior climatic conditions and healthful environment of the poor in Colorado, make Fresh Air work unnecessary." The secretary of the Associated Charities of Omaha says: "No such work carried on in our city, in fact our city is so open, has six parks, and very healthy, that such work is not considered necessary." Another writes of a Western town, "We have no tenement houses. As a rule each family occupies one house." From San Francisco comes the answer: "There are no Fresh Air Societies in San Francisco—the climate is cool and fresh the year round." The replies are significant. They confirm the impression made by a survey of the localities where the work abounds, namely, that this charity finds its expression almost entirely east of the Mississippi—St. Louis and Minneapolis being the exceptions. As population grows more dense and our cities become the seat of manufacturing as well as of commercial interests, the philanthropy flourishes. The principal cities of the Eastern Seaboard maintain large benevolences of this sort. Doubtless the great influx of foreign population into these cities has given a decided impetus to the work. Statistics touching the nationality of "Fresh Air Children" are almost entirely wanting, but there is scarcely room for doubt that the majority of the beneficiaries of the general societies are of foreign parentage.[1]

By reference to the location of the charities enumerated below, the Fresh Air agencies reported are seen to be distributed among 24 cities[2] and in 13 States.

	City and State.	Society.	Date
1	Albany, N. Y.	City Tract and Missionary Society	1891
2	Allegheny City, Pa.	Young Women's Christian Association	1890
3	Baltimore, Md.	Orange Grove Children's Country Home	1886
4	Baltimore, Md.	Children's Fresh Air Society	1891
5	Baltimore, Md.	Hollywood Children's Summer Home	1892
6	Baltimore, Md.	Hopewell Summer Home	1894
7	Boston, Mass.	Country Week	1875
8	Boston, Mass.	City Missionary Society	1880
9	Boston, Mass.	Children's Island Sanitarium	1886
10	Boston, Mass.	Episcopal City Missionary Society	1888
11	Boston, Mass.	Boston Institute Seashore Home	1888

[1] There is abundant proof of this in the work of the Children's Aid Societies of New York and Brooklyn, the Floating Hospitals of New York and Boston, and the character of the population in the fields where the general societies are chiefly engaged.

[2] Including New York City.

	City and State.	Society.	Date.
12	Boston, Mass.	Boston Floating Hospital	1894
13	Brooklyn, N. Y.	Children's Aid Society	1876
14	Brooklyn, N. Y.	Working Women's Vacation Society	1884
15	Buffalo, N. Y.	Fresh Air Mission	1888
16	Buffalo, N. Y.	Fresh Air Mission Hospital	1893
17	Chicago, Ill.	Daily News Fresh Air Fund	1887
18	Chicago, Ill.	Lake Geneva Fresh Air Association[1]	1888
19	Chicago, Ill.	Hinsdale Fresh Air Home	1891
20	Cincinnati, Ohio	Fresh Air Society	1886
21	Cleveland, Ohio	Children's Fresh Air Camp	1889
22	Detroit, Mich.	Association of Charities	1895
23	Hartford, Conn.	Charity Organization Society[2]	1894
24	Hartford, Conn.	City Missionary Society	1894
25	Indianapolis, Ind.	Summer Mission for Sick Children	1890
26	Milwaukee, Wis.	Associated Charities	1888
27	Minneapolis, Minn.	Minneapolis Outing Association	1890 a
28	New Haven, Conn.	City Missionary Association	1882
29	Philadelphia, Pa.	Children's Country Week Association	1877
30	Philadelphia, Pa.	Sanitarium Association	1877
31	Pittsburg, Pa.	Association for Improving the Condition of the Poor[3]	1879
32	Portland, Me.	Fresh Air Society	1890
33	Rochester, N. Y.	Infants' Summer Hospital, Ontario Beach	1887
34	Salem, Mass	Associated Charities	1892
35	Scranton, Pa.	Men's Guild of St. Luke's Church	1893
36	St. Louis, Mo.	St. Louis Republic[4]	1880
37	Worcester, Mass.	City Missionary Society	1895

This is the summary:

New York 5	Illinois 1	Minnesota 1
Pennsylvania 4	Indiana 1	Missouri 1
Massachusetts 3	Maine 1	Wisconsin 1
Connecticut 2	Maryland 1	
Ohio 2	Michigan 1	

The Nature of the Societies Doing the Work.

An interesting question arises at this point. What is the char-

a Approximate.

[1] "For poor children residing in or near Chicago."

[2] Money was raised by Hartford Courant (1894); Hartford Times (1895).

[3] The work of the Pittsburg society has passed through various forms. Owing to its changing character no statistics are presented previous to 1895.

[4] The "Protective Society for Women and Children" is in charge of the excursions. St. Louis supported a "Country Week" society (1884-1893), sending an average of 75 children a season to private families, at a total expense of $2,000.

acter of the organizations prosecuting this philanthropy? Have they been called into existence to cover a field neglected by older charitable enterprises, or is this relief work a branch of the general endeavor of these organizations? Is the impulse to Fresh Air activity born of religious motives, or is it humanitarian and secular in character? Is the church or the press the real dynamic agent in the movement? The answer is at hand in the very names of the societies themselves. The questions are not mutually exclusive. Each is found to be answered in the affirmative by a glance at the preceding table. Distinctly Fresh Air societies are in the majority. Some of these to be sure maintain a permanent office force and find work of an auxiliary character sufficient to occupy them during the winter. Others in the autumn, "fold their tents like the Arabs, and as silently steal away." Abounding with activity in the summer months, they hibernate the rest of the year. Good examples of the latter type are found in the Children's Country Week Association of Philadelphia, and the Fresh Air Society of Cincinnati, as the writer has occasion to know from his attempts to discover their winter quarters.

On the other hand, there are many permanent organizations which have undertaken the charity as a branch of their general work. Often these are missionary or similar societies born of religious enthusiasms. The seventy-ninth annual report of the City Missionary Society, of Boston, for instance, shows that 29 per cent. of the entire receipts of the society for 1895 were for its Fresh Air work.[1] Again, no one can have failed to observe the activity of the press in championing the charity. Its columns are always open to appeals for funds and not a few Fresh Air societies owe their support, if not their origin, to the influence of some particular paper. The largest Fresh Air work in the country carries the name of a well-known New York newspaper. The success of the Chicago Daily News and the St. Louis Republic in raising money for single day's outings is shown by the returns from their respective cities. This is not the place to speak of certain dangers to the work arising from indiscriminate newspaper appeals. One or two recent illustrations of this kind may be referred to later. An analysis of the societies doing general Fresh Air work, including the 14 similar agencies of New York City, exhibits this grouping:

[1] Received for missionary operations, $19,645.85. Contributions for relief work, $12,962.50. Contributions for Fresh Air Fund, $13,430.37.

Fresh Air Societies (distinctively)[1] 29
Missionary Societies 6
The Press 5
Organized Charitable Societies 4
Associations for Improving Condition of Poor 2
Children's Aid Societies 2
Churches 2
Christian Associations 1

Total[2] 51

The enumeration is unfair to the religious societies in one marked respect. By the very method of classification all sectarian societies are excluded. The activity of the churches, as shown in New York City alone, will serve to correct any false impressions on the subject.

Rise and Development of the Charity.

The first Fresh Air work of which we have authentic record was inaugurated by Rev. William A. Muhlenberg in connection with his own parish in New York City. Dr. Muhlenberg's biographer, Miss Anne Ayres, speaking of the clergyman's relation to the philanthropy, says: "The term Fresh Air, as applied to country refreshment for the poor in summer, and now so common amongst us, that many and various agencies for the purpose, have adopted the phrase, was original with Dr. Muhlenberg, both as to name and fact." Miss Ayres quotes from the rector's parish notes of the summer of 1849, showing that the Doctor began then to send people away on excursions. "A year or two later," continues Miss Ayres, "the Fresh Air provision became an established summer charity of the Church of the Holy Communion, and was often extended by the tender and loving pastor to other than its own church people. There is extant a debit and credit account of the 'Fresh Air Fund,' a year or two later, showing its benefits at an expenditure of about seventy dollars distributed thus: 'Two poor shirt sewers and consumptive brother, three weeks' board at Catskill; poor student in ill health, the same for over a month; an unhappy wife and two young children, and a widow and two young children, nearly two weeks; an old

---

[1] Among these 29 are a few, like the Country Week, of Boston, that are affiliated with all-the-year-round organizations. The Country Week is really an integral part of the Boston Young Men's Christian Union, although it has its own secretary and appeals to the public for support in its own name.

[2] The working girls' vacation societies, as well as the churches of New York City, are considered to be in a class by themselves.

man of eighty-five, his grand-children and great-grand-children, frequent trips to Staten Island; the same from time to time, to a poor old weaver, a sick and lonely widow, a lame boy, and some mothers with their sick infants.'" These were parishioners and most of the adults were communicants of the church. Here then is a beginning of Fresh Air work under ecclesiastical auspices.[1]

The organization of the General Fresh Air Societies was to come considerably later. A comparison of the dates at which these societies were severally constituted will show the recent character and rapid development of this form of the philanthropy. The table which follows gives the data on this point for the 51 general societies in existence in 1895, for which we have statistics.

Date of Organization.	No. of Societies Organized.	Date of Organization.	No. of Societies Organized.	Date of Organization.	No of Societies Organized.
1874	2	1884	1	1894	5
1875	1	1886	4	1895	2
1876	1	1887	3		
1877	4	1888	5		
1879	1	1889	1		
1880	2	1890	8		
1882	2	1891	4		
		1892	3		
		1893	2		
1874-1883 13		1884-1893 31		1894-1895.... 7	

According to the earliest of these dates general Fresh Air charity in the United States is not yet of twenty-five years' standing. That this is the fact there is good reason to believe, although the initial impulse to the work antedates 1874 by one or two years.

In an editorial in the New York Times of July 3, 1872, entitled, "Pity the Poor Children," the situation at that period is described and measures to provide immediate relief are urged.

"The heat burst upon us before many families had time to leave the city, and for nearly a week we have been living in an atmos-

[1] "The Life and Work of William Augustus Muhlenberg, D. D.," by Anne Ayres; New York, 1880; pp. 208-210.
In 1873, Dr. Muhlenberg opened a "summer retreat for poor children and weary mothers," at St. Johnland, Long Island. A farm house was bought by Mr. William H. Aspinwall and presented to Dr. Muhlenberg for this work. This "Cove House" has been called the "Mother House of all the 'Summer Homes.'" (Rev. J. Newton Perkins, *The Churchman*, Vol. LXXIV., No. 11, Sept. 12, 1896.)
The present Summer Home of the Church of the Holy Communion, at Ashford Hill Retreat, is now under the management of the Tribune Fresh Air Fund.

phere such as is experienced in July in the plains of Lower Bengal. . . From our office windows we can see, any night, scores of poor little waifs and strays, lying about in the City Hall Park, where, perhaps, they have been brought by some elder sister or kindly neighbor, in the hope of getting a breath of fresh air. It is enough to make the heart bleed to look at their white faces, and to listen to their sorrowful moans. . . . If excursions to the country or seaside could be arranged for the poor children, it would be the best possible plan of enabling them to withstand the stress of the present season. It would not cost much to give a hundred children a happy day. Indeed, if some one would but organize the work, there are thousands of our citizens who would gladly give five or ten dollars each toward sending a party of children into the country for a week at a time. The pleasure thus given to the neglected little ones would be incalculable and scores of lives would be saved."

The Times was urged to carry out its own suggestion. Accordingly, consultations were held with the managers of industrial and charitable schools of the city, and a plan of systematic procedure arranged. The city was districted and visitation provided for. The Times of July 10, said: "Besides the series of excursions already projected, we propose to expend a portion of the money sent us in providing sick children with many desirable luxuries." The Times continued its free excursions for three years. At the close of the season of 1874, it said of the work: "It must be remembered that the charity has this year been largely supplemented by the efforts of private societies, which now arrange excursions on their own account. . . . It is probable that, in future years, the work will fall more and more into the hands of private societies." Subjoined is the record of the excursions:

Year.	Children.	Adults.	Expenditures.
1872	18,672	1,723	$10,634.97
1873	21,393	775	9,640.40
1874	23,847		8,850.83
Total	63,912	2,498	$29,126.20

The receipts for the first year were $19,296.75. $5,183.04 was used in ministering to sick children in their own homes. 62,458 families were visited the first summer. The example of the Times was quickly followed in other places. Brooklyn and Philadelphia were among the first cities to organize similar excursions in 1872.

Among the several claimants for the honor of being the pioneers in Fresh Air relief stands St. John's Guild.[1] The Guild was founded in 1866 as a charitable relief society of St. John's Chapel, Trinity Parish.[2] It was one of the first societies to coöperate with the Times in arranging for district visitation among the sick children of its own parish.[3] In 1873, the Guild hired a barge and gave two excursions for sick children on its own account. In 1874, the society broke away from denominational control. Its activity, therefore, as a non-sectarian body dates from that year. The first summer of its independence the Guild provided 18 excursions for 15,202 sick children, and its receipts were $32,624—more than twice its entire revenue for the previous seven years of its history.

In 1874, Mrs. A. P. Stokes, Jr., who had maintained on Staten Island the previous summer a sanatorium for infants and poor children, passed over the enterprise into the hands of the Children's Aid Society.[4] The result of its first season's work is thus summed up: "Our experience last year showed us that the poor were at first exceedingly suspicious and distrustful of this kindness, many of them suspecting some project of proselytizing, or 'kidnapping' under it. The children themselves, too, became homesick after three days, and all very naturally had a special longing for bathing in hot weather."[5]

Accordingly, in 1875, quarters were rented at Bath Beach, L. I. It was not until several years later, that the society came into possession of its present properties at Bath and West Coney Island.

The Country Week, of Boston, was founded in 1875 by Rev. William C. Gannett with the assistance of his sister, Mrs. Kate Gannett Wells. Mr. Gannett drew his inspiration from reading of a similar experiment in Copenhagen. The first summer, 160 children enjoyed, on the average, a ten days' visit to the country. "About half this number went, like any other guests, directly into private families; the other half were cared for in three 'homes' extemporized for the purpose." In 1877, the management of Country Week was placed in the hands of the Boston Young Men's Christian Union, where it has since remained. The following year, the society included within its functions the payment of the traveling expenses of those who might receive invitations to visit their own friends in

[1] Monthly Bulletin of St. John's Guild, Vol. I., No. 10.
[2] Ibid., Vol. IV., No. 7.
[3] New York Times, July 19, 1872.
[4] Twenty-second Annual Report, C. A. S., 1874, p. 35.
[5] Twenty-third Annual Report, C. A. S., 1875, p. 33.

the country—invitations which otherwise must go unaccepted. Since that time the work of the Country Week has regularly fallen under three heads: "Boarded," "Invited," "Visited Friends."[1]

It was also in 1875 that the foundations of the future work of the Children's Country Week Association, of Philadelphia, were laid. In that year, Mrs. Eliza S. Turner took a few poor children into the country to visit for a week. "In 1877 the work commenced in earnest, and 59 children were sent away. In 1878, 238 were sent, and in 1879 the number had increased to 676; about one-half of the latter had been entertained free among the farmers and a small board paid for the rest."[2]

It would appear that the first organization to possess a "Summer Home," erected for the special purpose, was the Brooklyn Children's Aid Society. The matron of the society's present Home, Mrs. Douglas, who has been acquainted with its Fresh Air Work from the beginning, writes: "The Home was established in 1876, and grew out of the need of it made more evident, in benefit to sick babies, from a single day's excursion to the seashore; these excursions having been made under the auspices of the Children's Aid Society for several years previous. The first Home (1876) was erected for this work at West Brighton, Coney Island. . . . In 1886 our present buildings were erected and occupied the same year."

Of all Fresh Air philanthropies, none is better or more favorably known than that which for so many years has gone under the name of the Tribune Fresh Air Fund. This charity is largely the creation of one man—Rev. Willard Parsons. Mr. Parsons was pastor of a church in Sherman, Pa., when he persuaded some of his parishioners to receive into their homes as guests for a fortnight's vacation, the children of city tenements. This was in 1877. Sixty were thus entertained. The New York Evening Post fostered the enterprise during the next four years. In 1882 the work came under the auspices of the Tribune, whose name it has since borne.

From 1877, dates the work of both the Philadelphia Sanitarium Association and that of the Sanitarium for Hebrew Children of New York City. Free excursions for the day for poor children and their caretakers constituted for many years the work of these two societies.

---

[1] "Country Week," William I. Cole, New England Magazine, Vol. XIV., No. 5.
[2] Annual Report of the Association.

From a comparison of these dates, Fresh Air charity appears to have been decidedly in the air during the seventies. It is impossible to demonstrate that the various agencies which entered upon the work at that time drew their inspiration from a common source or were directly dependent one upon the other.[1] Doubtless such a connection is traceable here and there. But the very variety in form and method characterizing the Fresh Air relief goes to show that these early endeavors were more or less spontaneous movements animated by a common *zeitgeist*. If, however, the philanthropy is to claim descent from a single ancestor, Dr. Muhlenberg may well be considered its father. The work which he inaugurated in the Church of the Holy Communion is the first systematic effort to give Fresh Air refreshment of which we have record, and gave to the charity that form which has made so warm a place for itself in the heart of the church, especially of his own communion. Of the more general Fresh Air movements, the Times represents the Fresh Air excursion; the St. John's Guild, the Floating Hospital idea; the Children's Aid Societies of New York and Brooklyn, are the early representatives of organized colonization; the Country Week societies of Boston and Philadelphia, have emphasized the boarding-out system; while Mr. Parsons has been the champion of free entertainment.

[1] Reference has been made (p. 17) to the indebtedness of the Country Week, of Boston, to an earlier work in Copenhagen.

In Switzerland, Rev. W. Bion, of Zurich, in 1876, established the first of the Vacation Colonies. ("Zum XXjährigen Bestand der Ferienkolonien. Bericht von Zürich, 1895, von W. Bion, Pfarrer.") In 1895 Switzerland had 73 of these colonies to which 2,199 children were sent that year. The total number of children so cared for in twenty years was 21,734. ("Die Ferienkolonien für arme Schulkinder in der Schweiz, von Harald Marthaler." Bern, 1897.) The Swiss societies also conduct what are called Half-Colonies or Milk-Cures ("Die Halbkolonien oder Milchkuren"). The latter consist of children who are provided in their own homes morning and evening with milk and bread. Excursions and games are frequently allied features of the half-colonies. Over 25,000 children have enjoyed the privileges of the milk-cures. The statistician of this work in Switzerland, Rev. Harald Marthaler, says of the Vacation Colonies: "Provision for poor children during vacations had been made even before 1876. The significance of the movement which Rev. W. Bion instituted in Zurich, consists, however, in this, that the provision for vacations from that time was brought into systematic and very close relation to the public schools and conducted in strict adherence to pedagogical principles. For this reason it has developed into a philanthropy in the true sense—a philanthropy which claims the interest of all instructors, humanitarians, and hygienists, and is worthy the most unselfish affection of all good people and deserving of the sacrifices which have been made in its behalf." (Ibid, p. 3.)

The organized Fresh Air work of Germany is contemporaneous with that of Switzerland. It was in 1874 that the first Children's Sanatoriums

Number of Beneficiaries.

There are at least two standards by which Fresh Air societies attempt to measure their work. One of these is expressed by the number of their beneficiaries; the other, by their expenditures, total and per capita. To make the figures representing the first of these large, and those representing the second small, is a natural ambition. To do the largest possible business at the smallest pro rata cost is considered proof of good management in mercantile affairs. Why not in charitable work? But is it always desirable in relief work to do as large a business as possible? And what is a large business? And what is economy in Fresh Air charity? Where and how is the standard of measurement to be found? Where, if not by a comparison of actual results as reported by the different societies? How, if not by striking an average, however crude, from the societies' own records?

One of the chief purposes of a statistical study is the exhibition it affords of comparative results. The report of a single Fresh Air agency is an object of special interest to the members of its own constituency, while to say that those engaged in any form of philanthropy should acquaint themselves with the experiences of their fellow workers sounds like a platitude in these days of conference and coöperation. The writer has found in certain quarters a distinct distrust of statistical measurements and a consequent disinclination to try to reduce high ideals to the vulgar level of arithmetical expression. Yet it may be well to remind ourselves of the advantages and of the limitations of statistics. While the science may be quite inadequate to gauge moral motive or human happiness, none will deny its competency to deal with things material. Statistics is nothing more nor less than a method of scientific bookkeeping by which the community in its various social aggregates takes account of stock and estimates its gains and losses. No busi-

---

were opened in Kolberg and Rothenfelde. In 1876 the first children were sent to Vacation Colonies. In twenty years 300,000 children, in round numbers, have been cared for at an expense of about fifteen million marks. ("Bericht über die am 8. u. 9. August, 1896, in Berlin abgehaltene fünfte Konferenz der Vertreter von Vereinigungen für Sommerpflege." Berlin, 1896.)

For a brief summary of Fresh Air work in the various countries, see Marthaler's "Die Ferienkolonien, etc.," above quoted.

There are two things which stand out as characteristic of Fresh Air work on the Continent: (1) The marked coöperation of Fresh Air agencies by means of conferences and the exchange of reports; (2) the affiliations of the work with that of the public schools.

ness house can dispense with systematic accounting. No charitable enterprise can afford to neglect the same.

Before, however, we can safely compare the work of one society with another, it is necessary to analyze the data at hand with considerable care. There is no virtue in any column of figures whose only common property is the use of the same digits. In almost every case where the total number of beneficiaries is given, the datum is "official," that is, returned by the society itself. Not infrequently an organization has been able to furnish only the approximate information desired. This fact is indicated in the tables by the letter a placed against the figures in question. In a few instances we have been obliged to make our own estimates based on other official data. Similarly, the letter   is used to denote the fact. Where sufficient material is not available for an approximately accurate estimate, no figures are offered. But after all has been said any number representing simply the "total beneficiaries" is liable to mislead. Fresh Air societies, as we shall have occasion to see later on, are of two kinds. One type, reporting by far the larger number of persons, sends its beneficiaries away for a day at a time. Its work may be classed under the head of day excursions. The second type, reporting fewer individuals, but often actually furnishing a larger number of days' outings, is represented by the agencies which send their beneficiaries to the country or seashore for a series of days or weeks. In the first case, "total beneficiaries" will include many of the same individuals taken more than once, while in the second case, it will include many days' outings for the same individual. Therefore, not until the number which stands for "total beneficiaries" has been multiplied by the missing factor representing the number of days' outings which each person received, is it possible to compare intelligently the volume of Fresh Air work done by the different agencies. In short, the safe unit of measurement is not "beneficiaries" but "days' outings." Unfortunately, comparatively few societies reduce their work to this basis.[1] Most of them are content to give the average number of days for which their beneficiaries are sent, an average, by the way, which is apt to be quite as large as the facts will warrant.

Except in the case of New York City, where more diligent inquiry was possible, no attempt has been made to reduce the "total beneficiaries" of the general Fresh Air societies in the United

[1] The annual reports of the "Country Week," of Boston, are noteworthy exceptions.

States to "total days' outings." Probably, in most instances, it might have been safely assumed that the character of the several societies' work had remained constant. By taking, then, the average number of days' outings furnished to each individual in 1895 as a standard, it would have been a simple matter of arithmetic to have obtained the desired result, namely, total days' outings. It has seemed better on the whole to let the data stand as given—a striking example of incomplete analysis—and to depend for actual comparison upon the more accurate returns for 1895. That the distinction noted above in the types of work is not always remembered, even by the societies themselves finds a good illustration in the official returns made by one of them. "We have done a larger work than any we know of in the country," writes this particular society. This opinion is evidently based on the total number of its beneficiaries—a very large one, though not so large as that of some other agencies. The moment the activity of the society in question is measured by days' outings or total expenditures there are found to be several Fresh Air philanthropies that take precedence.

A further illustration of the need of an intelligent understanding of just what Fresh Air statistics mean in any given case, is furnished, if we compare what has been accomplished by two societies that conspicuously stand for the two types of work, namely, day excursions and country week, respectively. While each of the societies referred to, is, as a matter of fact, now interested in both types of the charity, each, nevertheless, lays special emphasis upon the one form or the other. The Philadelphia Sanitarium Association and what is now the Tribune Fresh Air Fund are contemporaneous, both having begun work in 1877. The latter has the advantage, in that Mr. Parsons has statistics of his beneficiaries from the beginning, while the Sanitarium Association has no records for its first two years. Since Mr. Parsons' work was comparatively small at the start, the advantage is really immaterial. The Philadelphia Sanitarium reports by far the largest number of beneficiaries of any society, nearly a million and a half persons. The total for the Tribune is 306,619. Has then the one agency done five times the work of the other? So it would appear, if the comparison were carried no further. More careful analysis, however, discovers the fact that the one agency confines its attention chiefly to the excursion type of charity and that the other lays special stress upon the country week form of the philanthropy. When the statistics of both organizations are reduced to a common denominator of days' outings, we find that the agency which had nearly five times as many beneficiaries as its fellow, provided but three-fourths as many days' outings.

The illustrations might be continued in the case of the Chicago Daily News and the Country Week, of Boston, but enough has been said to show the incompleteness of such a composite number as "total beneficiaries" for the purposes of intelligent comparison.

Total Expenditures.

Probably few people realize the amount of money annually expended for Fresh Air relief. The questions arise, Is this money wisely spent? Are Fresh Air funds economically administered? How far will a dollar go in this work? What is its influence upon its recipient? Does the shadow which haunts every other form of charitable endeavor, also lurk here—that of pauperizing those helped?

Evidently if it is always dangerous to give something for nothing, the more that is given under such circumstances, the greater the peril involved. On the other hand the less that is given, except in the case of utter destitution, the less necessary would it seem to be to give anything. But is Fresh Air charity open to the charge of giving something for nothing? And could the little that it costs per capita be contributed by those who are now the recipients? Statistics alone cannot answer all these questions, although the science may throw some light on them. What has been said about the inadequacy of the number representing total beneficiaries when taken alone, applies in a certain measure to total expenditures. One disturbing factor entering unequally or not at all into the cost of conducting the several charities, is the construction account. Many societies maintain no summer homes. Others at no expense to themselves have been presented with such homes, while some have erected permanent quarters out of current funds.

The effort has been made to distinguish carefully between building and operating expenses. It will be remembered that question No. 5, of the circular letter, distinctly asked for total expenditures, "excluding construction expenses." But every society has its own method for distributing the items of cost between the two accounts. Here is one that aims to keep its running expenses as low as possible. Its interpretation of the term construction, enables it to charge off to that account, items which another society includes under the head of operating expenses. Then by combining two classes of beneficiaries—day excursionists and country week visitors—it is able to present an exceedingly low figure for per capita cost, and to exclaim in its successive annual reports: "Surely this is an economical charity." The fact is, that few Fresh Air charities have spent money so generously on buildings and equipment, probably because few have had such wealthy patrons. Here is another society that represents in its financial statement an opposite extreme. Until very recently the organization held no property. On the debit side of the account appear along with cost of superintendence, wages, transportation, food, rentals and taxes, also brokerage on its investments, and the cost of fairs conducted in its behalf. It is plain that between two such extreme cases, no reliable per capita or per diem average of expense could be struck. Another agency, in its annual reports, publishes a summary of its work for several successive years. The only clue to its total expenditures, however, is under the head of "contributions." Comparison with the audited account for any particular year shows that the balance carried over from one year to another is credited to the next year as "contributions." This method may serve to flatter the generosity of the public, since it swells beyond their true proportions, the annual receipts for the enterprise, but to this extent readers of the reports are liable to be misled. Obviously here, as elsewhere, it is necessary to distinguish the two types of the charity. Those societies that devote their energies to day excursions will be able to report the largest number of beneficiaries at the least per capita cost. Also as the number of these increases, we may expect a corresponding decrease in the pro rata expense.

In the case of societies of the country week type, much will depend upon the location of the place visited, its distance from the city and whether transporation be by rail or by boat; the relative number of those entertained under one roof; the proportion of caretakers to children; the quality and variety of the food; whether property is owned or rented; the form of hospitality, that is, whether the children are boarded out, colonized or received as invited guests; these and other factors have an important bearing upon the matter of expenditure. Sometimes, an item of expense will seem abnormally large, as where one society reports a charge of thirty dollars for transporting its children from the railroad station to its home, and seventy-five dollars, or 5 per cent. of its total income, for the cab hire of its visiting committee. Presumably local conditions furnish a better warrant for the disproportion than would appear at first sight. Naturally, where other things are equal, the smaller the country week society, the larger will be the expense per capita. But there is a false economy, as well as a true one, and the question of small organizations versus large ones must reckon with other considerations as well as the pro rata cost of the respective enterprises.

In conclusion, it is to be said that a study of the data of expenditure, and a comparison with the expense account of other forms of charitable effort, leaves the impression that nowhere else in the wide field of relief work is more had for the money than here.[1] A large amount of the labor performed in connection with the charity is of a voluntary character. Collecting moneys, gathering children, furnishing entertainment, are often done gratuitously. Many persons stand ready to give their services to the charity in summer for the simple return of board and lodging. Transportation companies give reduced rates, merchants contribute supplies or furnish them at wholesale prices. No state enterprise could do a similar work at so slight a cost. Executive expenses are often reduced to a minimum and sometimes guaranteed by patrons of the philanthropy. Seldom is the charity open to the charge of extravagance on the showing of its operating expenses. More often, one has reason to ask if economy in per capita expenditure is not sometimes secured by swelling unduly the number of beneficiaries; in other words, by attempting the work on too wholesale a scale, when, like charitable efforts in general, it should be undertaken with the exercise of careful discrimination.

The statistics of beneficiaries and expenditures ought to help us in answering the question here raised. Reference to pages 11 and 12, where the names of the societies under consideration are printed in full, will furnish a key to the initials employed in the following tables.

---

[1] Occasionally one meets with what looks like a decided exception. One society, for example, reports total beneficiaries 3,045, and total expenditures (excluding construction account), to date, $81,886.35. This society receives women who are willing and able to pay the cost of board—estimated for them at $3.00. The writer knows of two women of culture and means who were received on these terms last summer. Children are received free. 1,604 is the record for ten years. Even granting that a considerable part of the total expenditures was for construction—although reported otherwise—the fact remains that the per capita cost is excessive and that the charity should receive only such adults as cannot afford to pay full board elsewhere.

STATISTICS OF BENEFICIARIES AND EXPENDITURES.

	City and Society.	Total Number of Beneficiaries.	Total Expenditures.
1	Albany, C. T. M. S.	679	$6,077.77
2	Allegheny City, Y. W. C. A.	1,100a	6,000.00a
3	Baltimore, O. G. C. C. H.	2,634	21,465.50
4	Baltimore, C. F. A. S.	887	1,287.71
5	Baltimore, H. C. S. H.	596	2,065.22
6	Baltimore, H. S. H.	140	890.92
7	Boston, C. W.	44,348	190,559.11
8	Boston, C. M. S.	87,860[1]	144,059.07
9	Boston, C. I. S.	1,604[2]	
10	Boston, E. C. M. S.	20,000a	18,000.00a
11	Boston, B. I. S. H.	5,490	
12	Boston, B. F. H.	5,300	4,575.73
13	Brooklyn, C. A. S.	88,499[3]	176,998.00 p.e
14	Brooklyn, W. W. V. S.	7,754	13,334.22
15	Buffalo, F. A. M.	6,000a	20,000.00a
16	Buffalo, F. A. M. H.	240a	4,500.00a
17	Chicago, D. N. F. A. F.	290,144[4]	44,394.69[5]
18	Chicago, L. G. F. A. A.	3,451	26,433.97
19	Chicago, H. F. A. H.	700	2,600.00
20	Cincinnati, F. A. S.	9,678[6]	18,699.43
21	Cleveland, C. F. A. C.	250	10,000.00
22	Detroit, A. C.	140	200.00
23	Hartford, C. O. S.	4,400a	2,114.95
24	Hartford, C. M. S.	82	242.70
25	Indianapolis, S. M. S. C.	3,137	6,191.47
26	Milwaukee, A. C.	1,000 a	1,200.00 a
27	Minneapolis, M. O. A.		
28	New Haven, C. M. A.	12,000a	3,000.00a
29	Philadelphia, C. C. W. A.		
30	Philadelphia, S. A.	1,409,402	
31	Pittsburg, A. I. C. P.		
32	Portland, F. A. S.	1,800a	3,300.00a
33	Rochester, I. S. H.	529	28,000.00a
34	Salem, A. C.	214	1,964.76
35	Scranton, M. G. St. L. C.		
36	St. Louis, St. L. R.	500,000	30,000.00
37	Worcester, C. M. S.	581	405.93

a Approximate.
p.e Partly estimated.
[1] Has also distributed 484,011 street-car tickets and 44,691 round-trip harbor tickets.
[2] Children only. Women are admitted at $3.00 a week.
[3] As the agent, in Brooklyn, of the Tribune Fresh Air Fund, it has also sent some 60,000 women and children on day excursions and about 12,000 children to the country for a fortnight, through that Fund.
[4] The figures are for years 1890-1895, inclusive.
[5] For years 1890-1893, inclusive, reckoned on the basis of "contributions."
[6] From 1892 to 1895, 1,205 of the beneficiaries were day excursionists.

Age Classification.

One simple explanation of the strong hold which the philanthropy has taken upon the popular imagination, is the fact that it is assumed to concern itself with the sick baby and the young child —those morally and physically destitute through no fault of their own.[1] Associated from the beginning with the name of Fresh Air Charity is the picture of the tenement boy or girl revelling in country air or the pining infant revived by cool sea breezes. Is the representation true to life?

More important, however, than the verification of the popular fancy is another question upon which accurate age statistics would throw light. The danger, in relief work, of pauperizing morally those who are assisted physically, has already been alluded to. However it may be with the parents, infants in arms will scarcely distinguish the sterilized milk served gratis by a Fresh Air sanatorium from the every-day article bought at current rates by the family wage-earner. Both source and quality of Fresh Air benefactions are beyond the conscious calculations of the younger children. The same cannot be said of their older brothers and sisters. If a vacation in the country is to be had for the asking, or there is to be a free picnic nearer home, why should not they, as well as their neighbors, get the benefit of it? However far apart statistics and child psychology may be in definition, the manifestations of human nature are competent to furnish both sciences with material.

What do the figures show with respect to the relative numbers of adults and children sent away? Does the philanthropy continue to be a children's charity? The question may best be answered by a study of the latest returns available—those for 1895.

Of the 37 societies reported outside of New York City, 9 confined their charitable ministration to children. 4 of the 9 agencies were in Baltimore. 28 societies dealt with both adults and children. 10 of these organizations in the statistics given, do not classify their beneficiaries according to age. Here, apparently, is reason for thinking that Fresh Air charity may have ceased to be peculiarly for children. Let us examine more closely the following tables.

---

[1] "It is not for those who have brought their miseries upon themselves, that we appeal—not for the drunkard, the spendthrift, or the profligate; it is for the helpless who have done no one any wrong, who, in too many instances, are forsaken and friendless in the world, and whose sorrows appeal to us with tragic pathos for relief."—N. Y. Times, July 3, 1872.

STATISTICS FOR 1895.

	City and Society.	Adults.	Children.	Mixed.	Total.
1	Albany, C. T. M. S.	...	169	...	169
2	Allegheny City, Y. W. C. A.	200	300	...	500
3	Baltimore, O. G. C. C. H. ...	...	406	...	406
4	Baltimore, C. F. A. S.	...	480	...	480
5	Baltimore, H. C. S. H. ...	...	199	...	199
6	Baltimore, H. S. M.	...	93	...	93
7	Boston, C. W.	255	2,527	...	2,782
8	Boston, C. M. S.	...	...	9.170	9,170
9	Boston, C. I. S.	...	215	...	215
10	Boston, E. C. M. S.	70	100	2,500	2,670
11	Boston, B. I. S. H.	...	...	1,003	1,003
12	Boston, B. F. H.	...	...	3,500	3,500
13	Brooklyn, C. A. S.	1,818	4,094	...	5,912
14	Brooklyn, W. W. V. S. ..	68	54	181	303
15	Buffalo, F. A. M.	12	792	...	804
16	Buffalo, F. A. M. H.	...	80	...	80
17	Chicago, D. N. F. A. F. ...	30.169	68,108	...	98,277
18	Chicago, L. G. F. A. A. ..	164	338	...	502
19	Chicago, H. F. A. H.	...	...	162	162
20	Cincinnati, F. A. S.	342	602	580	1,524
21	Cleveland, C. F. A. C. ..	12	40	...	52
22	Detroit, A. C.	40	100	...	140
23	Hartford, C. O. S.	...	...	2,000 a	2,000
24	Hartford, C. M. S.	2	27	...	29
25	Indianapolis, S. M. S. C. ..	22	337	...	359
26	Milwaukee, A. C.	...	136	...	136
27	Minneapolis, M. O. A.	30	200	...	230
28	New Haven, C. M. A.	...	...	1,500	1,500
29	Philadelphia, C. C. W. A. .	...	...	20,948	20,948
30	Philadelphia, S. A.	46.934	127,547	...	174,481
31	Pittsburg, A. I. C. P.	...	...	1,160	1,160
32	Portland, F. A. S.	112	130	...	242
33	Rochester, I. S. H.	...	97	...	97
34	Salem, A. C.	28	33	...	61
35	Scranton, M. G. St. L. C...	32	43	...	75
36	St. Louis, St. L. R.	...	...	25,689	25,689
37	Worcester, C. M. S.	...	...	581	581
	Total................	80,310	207,247	68,974	356,531

STATISTICS OF FRESH AIR SOCIETIES. 29

STATISTICS FOR 1895. (Concluded.)

No. Sent for One Day.	No. Sent for more than One Day.	Average Stay.	Total Days' Outings.	Expenditures.	Where Sent.	
....	169	2 weeks	2,366	$1,399.22	Home	1
....	500	2 weeks	7,000	1,800.00a	Home	2
....	406	2 weeks	5,684	1,577.14	Home	3
....	480	2 weeks	6,720	701.98	Pri. Fam.	4
....	199	2 weeks	2,786	422.17	Home	5
....	93	2 weeks	1,302	723.35	Home	6
....	2.782	12 days+	34,021	12,712.29	Pri. Fam.	7
9,170	....		9,170	13,430.37	Excs. & Home	8
....	215	13 days+ a	2,826	3,400.00 p.e	Home	9
2,500	170	10 days	4,200	3,500.00	Excs. & H.	10
141	862	6 days	5,313	3,645.00	Home	11
3,500	....		3,500	3,342.73	Excursions	12
....	5,912	5½ days	32,516	8,172.54	Home	13
181	122	2 weeks	1,889	750.82	Families	14
....	804	2 weeks	11,256	2,500.00a	H. & P. F.	15
....	80	2 weeks.[1]	1,120	1,500.00a	Home	16
98,277	....		98,277	11,366.75	Sanatorium	17
....	502	2 weeks	7,028	4,345.82	Home	18
....	162	2 weeks	2,268	365.05	Home	19
580	944	17 days+[2]	16,701	4,663.72	H. E. & P. F.	20
....	52[3]		....	1,500.00	Camp	21
....	140	2 weeks	1,960	200.00	Pri. Fam.	22
2,000	....		2,000	466.50	Exc's.	23
....	29	2 weeks	406	110.85	Pri. Fam.	24
....	359	6½ days a	2,348	1,177.34	Home	25
....	136	2 weeks	1,904	235.00	Home	26
30.t	200 a	2 weeks	2,830	200.00	H. & P. F.	27
1,500 a	....		1,500	336.53	Exc's.	28
16,000 a	4,948	1 week	54,636	16,000.00 a	P. F. & Exc.	29
174,175	306	1 week	176,317	12,623.96	Sanatorium	30
437	723	1 week	5,498	3,275.49	Home	31
....	242	1 week	1,694	654.00	Pri. Fam.	32
....	97	9 days[4]	880	1,750.00	Home	33
....	61	2 weeks+	861	680.92	Pri. Fam.	34
....	75	2 weeks	1,050	454.61	Home	35
25,689	....		25,689	2,048.08	Exc's.	36
450	131	2 weeks	2,284	405.93	Pri. Fam.	37
334,630	21,901	9.27 days	537,800	$122,438.16		

[1] Later information leads us to think this an underestimate.
[2] Exact total, 2,303 weeks.
[3] Retained till convalescent.
[4] 30 were sent for one week and 67 for ten days.

A comparison of totals in the foregoing tables, shows adults, 22.5 per cent.; children, 58.1 per cent.; and mixed or unclassified, 19.3 per cent. There were 80,310 adults to 207,247 children, or about two adults to five children. Our final conclusion as to the actual proportion of one to the other, prevailing throughout the charity as a whole, will depend upon the composition of the 19 per cent. unclassified. Have we any means by which these 68,974 persons, set down as "mixed," can be distributed among the adults and children with approximate accuracy? Three of the societies whose combined totals make up 80 per cent. of the beneficiaries classified as mixed, are known to deal chiefly with children. One of these, the St. Louis agency, declares the ratio of its own work to be one woman to five children. We think of no similar work where the proportion of adults is so small. Probably it is easily within bounds to say that the general ratio sustained on the average for the thirty-seven societies was one adult to two and a half or three children, say, four adults to eleven children.

One other thing remains to be considered, and that is, the relation of many of these adults to the children. As a matter of fact, they are very frequently present, chiefly in the capacity of caretakers. This is especially true in the case of the day excursions. Country week societies seldom depend upon parents to act as the guardians of their own children during the holiday. In the work of the Philadelphia Sanitarium Assocation, where the ratio is one adult to nearly three children, as well as on the excursions of the St. Louis Republic, the child is the center of interest.

In New York City, where we are able through more perfect records to classify all the beneficiaries of the general societies, with a single exception, 28.9 per cent. of these are adults. The St. John's Guild which alone receives more than half the adults reported, is distinctly a children's charity.

The foregoing analysis is sufficient to make it clear that so far, at least, as the general, non-sectarian societies are concerned, this philanthropy maintains its original character as the *children's* friend. The fact that so many of its wards are infants and very young children sufficiently accounts for the presence of so large a proportion of adults in the enumeration of total beneficiaries. Farther than this it is impossible to go with our age classifications. Fresh Air societies seldom attempt more than the rough distribution discussed above. In the case of country week societies which send children away for a prolonged holiday, the ages usually range from six or seven years to ten or twelve. It is often with the day excursionist that the greatest variety of ages is permissible. The adult caretaker is necessarily in evidence and her dependents range from the baby in her arms and the toddling youngster tugging at her skirts up to the "little mother" of ten or twelve.

A notable exception to the absence of specific age classification is afforded by the Philadelphia Sanitarium Association. This society is in the habit of summarizing its statistics for previous years under the heads: "Adults," "Infants under two years," "Between two and five years," "Between five and ten years," "Over ten years." In 1895 the proportions were as follows: Adults, 27 per cent.; infants under two, 17.6 per cent.; between two and five, 27 per cent.; between five and ten, 24 per cent.; over ten, 4 per cent. In the early days of the charity, the percentage of children over ten years of age was about ten per cent, or twice what it has been of late. The ratio of adults to children has ranged from one adult to less than three children at one time, to one of the former to four of the latter at another.

That all this is not a mere refinement of classification will appear from the light which such statistics shed upon a single question —the danger of pauperization. The last mentioned charity does its work by wholesale. The conditions of admission to its privileges are simple in the extreme. "Young children with proper caretakers on presenting themselves at the boat are taken without tickets or other requirements." What is the society's interpretation of the term—"young children?" The data are at hand for answering the inquiry. Only 4 per cent. of the children were over ten years of age, and nearly two-thirds of them were under five. The large proportion of very young children does much to save the philanthropy from the danger attendant upon free picnics of a more indiscriminate charity. How far parents, able to pay their children's way, take advantage of such generous provisions for daily river excursions, statistics cannot answer.

Sex.

Not much is to be said on this point. The proportion of boys and girls is less frequently noted than the ratio of adults to children. On the whole, girls seem to have a decided advantage over boys. That the former are the more amenable to discipline, especially within the age limits generally recognized by societies of the country week type, accounts for the discrepancy in their favor. Men are seldom a factor. The term "adults" for statistical purposes may be regarded as equivalent to "women."

Two Classes of Fresh Air Societies.

The misleading character of the number representing the "total beneficiaries" in this work, has been previously discussed. The inadequacy of the term, as already pointed out, arises from the fact that it fails to discriminate between the two types of Fresh Air relief. The total number of persons given outings in 1895 by the 37 societies under consideration was 356,531. How many of these enjoyed single-day excursions? How many were given a holiday in the country or at the seashore for several days or a fortnight? Our statistical returns, when properly distributed between the two classes of Fresh Air societies, will enable us to answer the query. While it is true that many agencies engage in both forms of the work, it is equally true that the one type or the other predominates in each case. It is not difficult, therefore, to fairly classify the societies. When the beneficiaries of the charity are thus distributed in the two groups: "Number sent for one day," and "Number sent for more than one day," the nature of the work in general, or that of any society in particular, is readily determined. Here, as in so many forms of philanthropy, the inquiry suggests itself whether it is better to do much for a few, or a little for many. Later it will be in order to discuss the relative advantages of the two types of relief. Just now we are concerned with the facts of the case—the actual number of day excursionists, and also of those who enjoyed the privileges of country week, the average length of holiday afforded the latter, and the relative proportion of societies and beneficiaries of the two classes.

Of the 37 Fresh Air societies enumerated outside the city of New York, only 6 would appear from the table to confine their attention to day excursions. Two of these, however, are known to provide for a few cases of the second type. 22 agencies report work of the country week type, while 9 furnish statistics referring to both classes of beneficiaries. These 9 again, may be distributed among the two types according to the proportion of days' outings actually furnished in the one case, or the other. But two of these 9 societies really belong to the first class. The result of the analysis, then, shows:

```
        Societies of the "Excursion" type ................. 8
        Societies of the "Country Week" type ............. 29
                                                          ──
            Total ....................................... 37
```

While thus the advantage in number of societies lies so decidedly with the country week form of the benevolence, the case is quite different in the number of beneficiaries of the two types. 334,630 was the number sent for a single day, against 21,901 sent for a longer period. It should be said that the former figure does not mean so many different individuals. Undoubtedly, there were many who enjoyed single day's outings several times over. The point is that the persons were not given lodging, but were returned to their own quarters at night, and were counted again when they were next sent away, although this might well be on the succeeding day.

How many distinct individuals compose these 334,630 day excursionists there is nothing to determine. It is quite possible that the aggregate of days' outings in many cases may have exceeded the average length of holiday provided by some of the country week societies. Sometimes what are practically season tickets are issued to specially deserving beneficiaries. Our statistical resources oblige us to regard the days' outings provided as the sole clue to the number of excursionists. With this qualification in mind, the data at hand may be said to show that more than fifteen times as many persons were sent for the day as were sent for a country visit. The distribution of these excursionists by cities is significant. Philadelphia, Chicago and St. Louis provided outings for nearly 300,000 of the entire number. It is the wholesale scale on which their three agencies of the first type operate, that establishes the great disproportion between the number of beneficiaries credited to the two classes of Fresh Air societies.

Judging from the geographical distribution of the charity, one might conclude that the country week type was the more in favor. 21 out of the 23 cities here enumerated report Fresh Air societies of the second class. New Haven and St. Louis are the two exceptions. On the other hand, 11 cities out of the 23 return 15 agencies as giving outings of the first type, but in 5 of the cities only is the day excursion the predominating type among these 15 societies.

The 21,901 beneficiaries belonging to societies of class II., received a total of 203,170 days' outings in 1895. This was an average of 9.27 days to each person. The averages reported by the individual organizations ranged from $5\frac{1}{2}$ days to "convalescence." The longest specified term was 17 days. The more usual length of stay was two weeks. 18 societies give holidays of this average duration. It has been assumed that the term "two weeks" always means a period of 14 days. There is reason to think, however, that in some cases the term is used rather for convenience than accuracy. Both the day of arrival and that of departure may be counted in the estimate, or those sent on a Monday may return on the second Saturday. Then again, vacancies occur before the expiration of the fortnight. Children grow homesick and are sent away, or are called home by trouble or sickness in their families. Other children may be sent to fill their places in the country. Probably both sets of children will be credited in the society's report with having enjoyed the average number of days' outings furnished to the other beneficiaries. These exaggerations are partially balanced by the fact that some societies keep special cases longer than the specified time. We have yet to find an instance where an organization has deliberately underestimated its work, statistically.

Notwithstanding what has been said, we need have no fear that the totals arrived at, exaggerate in any degree the volume of Fresh Air relief given in the country at large. For 37 agencies in 23 cities (not counting New York) to have provided half a million days' outings to the sick and destitute poor in a single year is no mean showing. Were we to add to these general Fresh Air societies the numerous churches and benevolent agencies which are actively at work in this field of philanthropy, an enlarged conception of the work would be obtained.

Cost per Capita, 1895.

A vital matter with any form of philanthropic endeavor is the expense account. Those forms of relief which deal with certain individuals of a particular group in society and which can be administered at not too great a cost per capita, may safely be left to private philanthropy. Yet the demands for assistance have at times proved so pressing and widespread, as to baffle the efforts of the generously disposed. Or again, an experiment undertaken by a company of benevolent individuals may have been so successful as to call for the adoption of its aims and methods by the State. If the time should ever come when the municipality should find it expedient to subsidize a scheme of summer outings for the children of the poor,[1] the experience of the voluntary Fresh Air societies would furnish valuable standards of comparison for the enterprise. Not the least

---

[1] There are signs that the wedge of state-help has already been inserted in behalf of Fresh Air charity. The line of least resistance is naturally found in the hospital work of the charity. In Boston, in 1896, the municipality assumed the expenses of a sanatorium for infants

important of these would be the limits within which expenditure may properly move. We may hope, however, that private philanthropy will continue to prove itself able to cope with the situation. The present drafts made upon voluntary Fresh Air agencies may be approximately ascertained by a study of the expenditures of the societies under consideration, for 1895.

It is assumed that in the statistics of expenditure for the current year as well as for previous years, only running expenses are included. Probably such is not always the case. Even if it were, there is here again the latitude of interpretation as to what properly may be considered running expenses. In the attempt to arrive at an approximate standard of comparison in the cost of this work, care must be taken to consider the two types of agencies, separately. The per capita expense for excursionists manifestly will not serve as a unit of measurement when considering the expense of sending children on a visit to the country.

First, as to the cost of day excursions. Even here we may be prepared to find a considerable variety in the range of expenditure on the part of individual societies. In 1895, St. Louis gave 25,689 women and children a day's outing at a total cost of $2,048.08. The number of excursionists was the greatest and the pro rata expense the smallest in the society's experience. The beneficiaries are transported by boat to the country, where the day is spent. "Children are selected by a paid visitor, through city missions and charitable organizations." The per capita expense as reported for 1895 was almost exactly 8 cents.

The Chicago Daily News Fresh Air Fund cared for 30,169 mothers, 47,551 children and 20,557 sick babies in 1895. The cost

which had previously been supported by voluntary contributions. The conduct of the enterprise still remained in private hands.
In 1894, the Legislature of the State of New York passed the following act, appropriating public funds:
"To St. John's Guild of the City of New York, the sum of thirty thousand dollars to be applied to the maintenance and operation of its hospitals, to the support of its other charitable work and to the general uses and purposes of said society, and to the Sanitarium for Hebrew Children in the City of New York, the sum of five thousand dollars to be applied to the support of its charitable work." (Laws of the State of New York, 1894, Vol. II., Chapter 501.)
St. John's Guild (Annual Report, 1894) finds cause for self-congratulation that the society had been "favored with a place in the lists of organizations deemed to be entitled to aid from the City Treasury in its charitable appropriations." In 1895, however, the management reported: "It is not without some discouragement that those in charge of the affairs of the Guild realize that the contributions to our funds have fallen off to an amount nearly equal to the city's aid."

of the work was $11,366.75. The beneficiaries as a rule get themselves to the Sanitarium, located on the Lake Shore of Lincoln Park. "There are no 'processes' or 'conditions' necessary to secure treatment." The food furnished is of the simplest character and much of it is donated by a single baking company. Four physicians, each for an hour a day, are in attendance at the Sanitarium, while three others are available for consultation. This service is voluntary. In addition, there is a house staff of four doctors and a corps of nurses regularly employed. The "hospital cases" numbered 3,533,—33 of whom died. The expenses of the executive management of this charity are met by the Daily News and were, in 1895, $3,386.09, while $7,980.66 were expended "on account of Lincoln Park Sanitarium." The per capita cost of the entire enterprise was 11½ cents.

The Philadelphia Sanitarium Association reports the largest number of beneficiaries of any Fresh Air agency—the enormous total of 174,481 persons. The operating expenses of the charity were $12,623.96. The following were the chief items of expense. Maintenance of the two steamers plying between the city and Red Bank, N. J., $5,616.74. Food supply, $1,270.09. Salaries and wages of Sanitarium staff, $2,457.14. The per capita cost was 7.2 cents. The transportation expense was a little more than 3 cents and the cost of food less than one cent for each individual. This average covers also the treatment of 179 hospital cases, who, with 127 caretakers, remained at the Sanitarium on an average, one week.

We have discussed these three forms of Fresh Air relief not so much for the purpose of comparison as to show how small the cost per capita may be made when distributed among a host of beneficiaries.

The Charity Organization Society of Hartford and the New Haven City Missionary Society both report approximately the same number of day excursionists. The per capita expense of the former was 23 cents, that of the latter 22 cents. The work of the Boston City Missionary Society is apparently an exception to this standard of economy. 9,170 beneficiaries classified as day excursionists are represented as having cost the society $13,430.37. The statistics are misleading. Thousands of tickets for street cars and harbor excursions were distributed by the organization and a hundred or more women and children sent on a visit to the society's own cottage in Maine.

The only other agency whose beneficiaries would appear to belong exclusively to the type of day excursionists is the Floating Hospital of Boston, where the cost per capita in 1895 was nearly $1.00. The plan of the work is similar to that of the New York society, whose example the Boston Floating Hospital is avowedly following. The greater proportionate expense of the latter's work is doubtless due to the difference in the scale of operations and the lack of permanent equipment.

Two conclusions may be drawn from the above analysis of expenditures for Fresh Air work of the first type. Much depends upon the character of the outing, that is, whether it is primarily recreational or recuperative. Hospital treatment will considerably enhance the cost of the philanthropy. On the other hand, no one factor is of such influence in reducing pro rata expenditure as doing the work by wholesale.

For the analysis of the expense account of country week societies, it is possible to select agencies which possess at least two features in common. 6 cities report 8 societies which entertain their beneficiaries in "Homes" for two weeks in each case.

City.	Beneficiaries.	Expenditure.	Average Per Week.	Average Per Capita.
Albany	169	$1,399.22	$4.13	$8.27
Allegheny	500	1,800.00 a	1.80	3.60
Baltimore:—				
Orange Grove	406	1,577.14	1.94	3.88
Hollywood	199	422.17	1.06	2.12
Hopewell	93	723.35	3.88	7.77
Chicago	502	4,345.82	4.32	8.65
Milwaukee	136	235.00	.86	1.72
Scranton	75	454.61	3.03	6.06
	2,080	$10,957.31	$2.63 av	$5.26 av

The analysis shows a wide range of expenditure, varying from $1.72 per capita for a fortnight's vacation to $8.65. The minimum is so small as to make it evident that there is a factor missing from the calculation. To be sure, transportation is free and much of the service voluntary, but on the other hand, rent is a fixed charge. The Albany society also pays rent. The Lake Geneva work is for both children and working girls. Transportation is a considerable item of expense. The variation in the expenditures of these eight societies is wide enough to make the average, $5.26 per capita, for two weeks' outing, of doubtful value as a unit of measurement.

We may compare with these figures the averages of certain of the New York societies. In 1895, the Tribune Fund maintained, at its own charges, two summer colonies. The Life Fund under the same management also conducted a large colony. Exclusive of cost of transportation the showing is:—

	Children.	Total Expense.	Per Capita for Two Weeks.
Tribune:—			
Ashford Hill Colony	1,099	$2,979.50	$2.71
Eunice Home Colony	475	1,613.49	3.39
Life's Farm Colony	1,180	3,935.79	3.33

If we attempt to reduce to the common denominator of a fortnight's outing the work of other New York societies supporting Summer Homes, the results, reckoned on the basis of their average *per diem* expenditures in 1895, are:—

Society.	Beneficiaries.	Average Cost per diem.	Making Estimated Average for Two Weeks.
All Souls'	600	$ .69	$9.66
Summer Shelter of Morristown	180	.62	8.68
Lana ne Tela Society	280	.40	5.60
Christian Herald Home	2,378	.37	5.18

The "personal equation" of each society, which will explain in a measure the variation in the averages as thus estimated, will be given in its proper place.

Quite as difficult is it to arrive at any fair estimate of the averages for societies which send their beneficiaries to private families, either as invited guests or as boarders. The Children's Fresh Air Society, of Baltimore, which relies upon free entertainment for its wards, reports for 1895 the per capita cost of a two weeks' outing as $1.49. The Tribune's averages vary from $1.83, the average cost per capita in 1892, when its work was at its maximum, to $3.55 in 1880, when not more than 2,500 beneficiaries were sent away. These figures represent chiefly traveling expenses.

Of the societies which pay board for their beneficiaries, the Hartford City Missionary Society reports its rate for children in 1896 as $2.00 a week, or $4.00 per capita for the fortnight. The Salem Associated Charities pay at the rate of $5.00 for children and $6.00 for adults for two weeks. The reports of the Boston Country Week show that the charge for board for two or three years past has been at the rate of about 40 cents a day, or $2.80 a week.

Enough has been said to show how variable a quantity, average per capita cost really is. We are forced to the conclusion that no exact standard or general average is obtainable from the data in hand. If the quest is unsuccessful where the conditions are most nearly alike, it is useless to attempt comparisons between societies engaged in both forms of the charity and in varying proportions.

The most that can be said is that each organization has its own individuality, its own "standard of living." Societies publishing annual reports usually include an itemized financial statement. This serves to show the conditions under which the work is carried on. In many instances, the practical policy adopted is to cut the Fresh Air coat according to the cloth. The resources of a society often seem to have quite as much to do with determining what form its Fresh Air relief shall take, as have any well thought out theories about the advantages of one form over another. In short, income plays a large part in deciding the nature and the extent of the philanthropy. Where resources are abundant, two dangers are present here as well as in other forms of charitable work. They are allied. One is often the cause of the other. The first is indiscriminate giving; the second, the creation of an artificial need. Any discussion of these points may well be reserved.

The Form of Entertainment.

Perhaps there is no point upon which the organizers of Fresh Air charity are more divided than upon the kind of hospitality that is best for their wards. Whatever the individual theories, it is worth while to observe the actual practice of the societies as a whole.

Where organizations adopt more than one method of entertainment, each will be counted separately as if it were the sole method employed. The classification, therefore, includes each form as often as it finds illustration in practice.

		Outside N. Y. City.	In New York.	Total.
Single day's outings	Sent on Excursions	8	7	17
	or			
	Received at Sanatoriums	2		
"Country Week" outings	At Homes [1]	22	13	35
	In Private Families	12	1	13
	Total	44	21	65

[1] One of the Homes is called a "Camp." The use of tents is unique.

The word sanatorium is used in this connection for charities which combine the excursion feature with medical treatment. The word Home is used as a general term to cover all degrees of "colonization" or the grouping of numbers of children at a given place. Each society is in control of the Home it occupies, either by virtue of purchase, gift, loan or rental. Sometimes these Homes partake of the character of children's nurseries or hospitals.[1]

Entertainment in private families may be of three sorts. Occasionally, beneficiaries are sent away to visit friends. Sometimes they go to strangers, as invited guests. More often they are boarded—frequently on farms. The Country Week, of Boston, which works entirely through families, thus distributed its beneficence in 1895:

Sent to friends	125	4.4 per cent.
Invited, as guests	356	12.7 per cent.
Boarded	2,301	82.7 per cent.

The Fresh Air Society, of Cincinnati, avails itself of both the private family and the Home. It gives these statistics for 1895:

Sent to friends	89	9.4 per cent.
Entertained at the Home	353	37.3 per cent.
Boarded on farms	502	53.1 per cent.

Of the 14 General Fresh Air Societies in New York City, the Tribune alone utilizes the hospitality of private families. Of late years, however, more and more of its own children have been sent to Homes. In 1895, the Tribune Fund availed itself of twelve such Homes.

Of the 8,000 children sent out by the Fund more than half were "colonized." Mr. Parsons' children, sent to private families, go either as invited guests or to their own relatives or friends in the country. The Fund does not pay board for its wards. The Children's Country Week Association, of Philadelphia, on the contrary, sends away the larger share of its beneficiaries as boarders. Except in the case of the Tribune and one or two of the smaller societies, "boarding out" seems the practice most in vogue among agencies utilizing family life rather than institutional influences. Statistics go to prove that in the case of Country Week societies, there are 35 instances where the children are colonized to 13 instances where

---

[1] It has not been feasible to attempt nice distinction between Fresh Air charities of the hospital type, and other forms. The two are so often combined or overlap that exact classification is impracticable. Only charities confining their activity to the summer are included.

they are sent into families, and that where the latter is the case, with the exception of the Tribune, the payment of board is the rule rather than reliance upon free entertainment.

Doubtless the exigencies of a rapidly growing charity have done much to shape both the method and structure of Fresh Air relief. It remains to discuss the relative merits of the various forms of the philanthropy. Before doing so, it will be in order to consider the charity as it exists in a single city, that of New York.

CHAPTER III.

FRESH AIR RELIEF IN NEW YORK CITY.

So far our attention has been chiefly confined to a bird's-eye view of Fresh Air charity in the country at large. In the study of the work as carried on in New York, a more complete description of its representative forms as well as fuller statistics will be practicable.

New York City offers a rich field for the investigation of Fresh Air Relief. The local conditions have been peculiarly favorable to the development of the charity. Here is an immense tenement-house population. Here, of all cities in the world, is the greatest density of population to an acre.[1] Here is peculiarly the birthplace of the American slum.[2] Here are hordes of recent immigrants huddled together in small national groups. The streets of the tenement sections swarm with children by day and by night. The stoop and the sidewalk are the recreation ground of mothers and their babies. The saloon or the "café" is the social club of fathers and sons. The fire escape and the roof afford refuge for those in search of fresh air denied them in their own ill-ventilated quarters.[3]

What wonder that such conditions have appealed to the generously disposed in a community where the rôle of Dives and Lazarus is daily enacted in real life. Thanks to a growing sense of municipal responsibility, eternal vigilance seems just now the motto of those entrusted with the sanitary protection of the city. The mortality of children under five years of age has steadily decreased since the organization of the Board of Health.[4]

---

[1] This statement is strictly true only for Manhattan Island. There are, however, districts more dense than any that are known to exist elsewhere. (See "Report of the Tenement-House Committee of 1894," pp. 10, 256, 257.)

[2] "According to the best estimates, the total slum population of Baltimore is about 25,000; of Chicago, 162,000; of New York, 300,000; of Philadelphia, 35,000." ("Seventh Special Report of the Commissioner of Labor, 1894," *The Slums of Great Cities*, p. 12.)

[3] One of the evidences of this is the number of deaths caused by falls from fire-escapes. From 1880 to 1895, there were 237 such fatalities, while for the first three quarters of 1896, there were 24, 17 of these being in the third or summer quarter. (Memorandum furnished by Dr. Roger S. Tracy, Register of Records, New York Health Department.)

[4] The Death-rate of children under 5, in 1870, was 119.9; in 1875, 115.9; in 1880, 104.4; in 1890, 99.0; in 1895, 86.5. Ibid.

Voluntary agencies have coöperated to the same end. One of the forms of private endeavor most in evidence is Fresh Air relief. So extensively has this summer charity developed that it is probably true to-day, that no sick baby need die for want of sea air and medical treatment, nor need any ailing child go without an outing in the country or by the ocean because the parent is too poor to provide it. Whether such a statement is within bounds, one may judge for himself after a review of the statistics on the subject. It can be true, of course, only on condition that the Fresh Air relief available be fairly distributed.

We have already alluded to the advantage which an inquiry like the present one has in such a city as New York. It is possible, for example, in this case, to collect data concerning the activity of the general Fresh Air societies from the beginning of their work. Many of these, to be sure, compile no comprehensive summaries, nor is there always a clear distinction drawn in the annual totals between day excursionists and weekly visitors. Rarely are total days' outings reported, except to give the average length of time for which it is customary to send beneficiaries. However, personal correspondence and interviews with the officers of the societies, together with a comparison of their reports, have made it possible to compile tables that are presented with considerable confidence in their essential accuracy.

Again, as has been said, an exhibition of the activity of churches and other agencies ministering to their respective constituencies, is quite possible within the area of a single city. Even here it has been necessary to rest content with the data of but one year.

A third form of the philanthropy, possessing certain unique features which put it in a class by itself, is the vacation society for working girls. This important branch of the charity is also made an object of special inquiry in New York City. The subject at this point, then, naturally divides itself into three parts:

I. General and Non-Sectarian Fresh Air Societies.
II. Parochial Fresh Air Agencies.
III. Working Girls' Vacation Societies.

The work of only the first of these three, may be fairly compared with the similar work already reviewed.

A brief description of the salient features of the work in its various forms may serve as an introduction to the statistical data.

There is scarcely any plan of operation known to the charity that is without representation in the work of the 14 General Societies here enumerated.[1] An account of their methods of procedure will, therefore, very well illustrate the *modus operandi* of Fresh Air work at large.

St. John's Guild.—In 1895, St. John's Guild had just passed its twenty-first birthday as an independent organization. The present methods of the Guild may therefore be regarded as the fruit of mature experience. The character of the larger part of its summer work is clearly indicated in the name of its huge barge— the "Floating Hospital." From the start, the society has singled out the sick child as its primary concern. During the hot months, the Floating Hospital makes six trips a week—weather permitting —to the Lower Bay. Physicians at the city hospitals and dispensaries, or at work among the poor, are supplied with tickets admitting to the privileges of the barge. Any poor mother with a sick baby or young child may avail herself of these tickets. Well children, too young to be left at home, are allowed to accompany their parents. The barge makes three landings along the river front, on each trip. One day the landings will be on the east side of the city, and the next day, on the west side.

The Guild's hospitality—using the word in its literal sense—is thus brought as close as possible to the doors of the poor. 1,500 persons may be comfortably cared for on each excursion. A physician from the Board of Health is in attendance, especially to guard against the admission of contagious diseases. If a case chances to run the gantlet of the examination at the dock, the hospital physician, who begins his rounds as soon as the boat heads for the harbor, is sure to detect it, and the child is isolated. The doctor and his staff of trained nurses note the needs of each family group and make prompt provision to meet them. The sickest babies are sent to the wards. Here they are deposited in comfortable cribs and assured special attention. Much reliance is placed upon the sea air as a tonic. The Floating Hospital is equipped with abundant bathing facilities. The babies first receive attention. Then come the younger children. The mothers also have their turn. Fresh washrags, as well as clean towels, are supplied for each bather. 11,043 salt water baths was the record of the hospital in 1895. A hot meal is served at noon to the adults and older children, and sterilized milk twice daily for the babies. The Floating Hospital's destination is New Dorp, Staten Island, where is located

---

[1] None of them in 1895 boarded its wards with private families in the country, although the Life Fund formerly did so.

the Guild's Seaside Hospital, capable of accommodating 300 patients. To this are transferred the more serious cases, with the mothers who are to assist in the care of their children. In this way, provision is made for more permanent treatment. It should be said, however, that many of those on the barge who cannot be spared from home over night, are given "season tickets" good for a succession of trips. A sick child may thus be taken on the water several times a week.

Not the least valuable feature of the work is the instruction given the mothers in the proper care of their infants. Bathing, preparation of food, reliance upon nature's restoratives as well as upon drugs—all these lessons are taught the mothers in this great floating clinic.

Children's Aid Society.—The New York Children's Aid Society is by no means solely a Fresh Air agency, yet in seeking to find ways in which to prove itself the children's friend, it was among the first to take up Fresh Air work as one instrument to carry out its purpose.

The society now maintains both a "Health Home" at West Coney Island, and a "Summer Home" at Bath Beach, L. I. To the former are sent young children and infants, more or less ailing, and their mothers. The work here is curative rather than recreational. At the Summer Home the children of its industrial schools receive a holiday of from one to six days. The first week after the Home is opened is devoted to picnic parties largely composed of the boys of the schools, the older of whom are not received as weekly guests. The latter are entertained from Monday until Saturday. This is the length of stay permitted also at the Health Home. If specially in need of a longer vacation, visitors may return for a second week.

The children at the Summer Home are supplied with various means of entertainment, such as swings, merry-go-round, camera obscura, gravity railroad, and abundant bathing facilities. Comfortably furnished quarters are provided where girls indisposed may take themselves away from their mates. Books and papers are at hand. Two features of the place impress the casual visitor as unique. One is the location of the bath-houses, which are on the second floor, over one of the dormitories. This arrangement economizes space and enables the ingenious superintendent, Mr. Fry, to carry out his theory that children's dormitories should be on the first floor to avoid all danger from possible panics. Another invention of the superintendent is the method of seating the children at their meals. Open circular tables, not unlike a horseshoe in general shape, are used for the purpose. A small table within the enclosure of the larger one, gives a place of deposit for the dishes from which the children are to be served. By seating the girls both within and without the horseshoe table, fifty are accommodated in a comparatively small space and the problem of helping them much simplified. The tables are of hard wood, highly polished. Cloths are unnecessary. Economy and neatness are both subserved, while the angularity so often seen in the dining arrangements of large institutions, is entirely absent.

While the Summer Home of the society is enjoyed chiefly by the wards of its own industrial schools, toward the close of the season room is found for children from some of the missions of the city. Mention must be made of the cottage provided for crippled girls, a group of whom spend several weeks at the Home, living out-of-doors and entering more or less into the life of the place. The preference of the superintendent as shown by the buildings more recently erected, is plainly for the "cottage system" over that of large dormitories. The effort is to de-institutionalize so far as possible, by breaking up into small family groups. That the cottage system may itself be carried to extremes, seems to find illustration at the Health Home of the society. In the effort to isolate family groups the difficulty of maintaining both peace and cleanliness, particularly among the more ignorant of the foreign born, has been enhanced. There is a happy medium in this matter which the society evidently appreciates and means to secure.

Sanitarium for Hebrew Children.—Although the St. John's Guild, the Children's Aid Society, and others of the General Fresh Air Societies in New York, know neither nationality nor creed in the exercise of their hospitality, it was to be expected that difficulties would arise, in the very attempt to disregard racial and religious distinctions. Especially is this true where Christians and Hebrews are entertained at the same time. The strict dietary laws of the orthodox Jew can scarcely be carried out except under the auspices of his own coreligionists. Originally the barge of the St. John's Guild was placed at the disposal of Jewish mothers and their sick children on certain days of the month. The arrangement proved inadequate. Although the Floating Hospital continues to carry hosts of Jewish children and their caretakers, provision is also made for such by the Sanitarium for Hebrew Children.

It was in 1877, that the foundation of the work under Hebrew auspices was laid, in a single excursion by water. The president of the society said at the dedication of the Sanitarium building: "During our brief existence over 125,000 persons have been under our care."[1] This was in 1892. Up to this time, reliance had been placed upon the benefit to be derived from day excursions. By the opening of a permanent building, the Sanitarium was able to develop its hospital work and to retain cases at its Home for several days' treatment.

The work of the society at present is of three kinds. Each week a water excursion is given to some grove where a landing is made. Music is furnished on these occasions. Physicians are in attendance to care for any sick ones. The excursionists are allowed to carry luncheons, but each basket is examined to see that the food is of a proper kind. In addition, the society provides for its wards a list of good things, such as milk, bread, sandwiches, cake and ice cream. The water excursions in 1895 carried on the average 737 persons, or a total of 6,632 mothers and children in the ratio of about 1 to 3. The per capita expense was $23\frac{1}{8}$ cents.

The Sanitarium kept open its building at Rockaway Park, from the middle of June to the middle of September. During these three months 803 patients were received. 51 ailments are cited in the report of the house physician. The layman may well echo the sentiments expressed to the writer by one of the officers of the society, that until he read the physician's report he did not know that there were so many children's diseases in existence.

Of the 803 persons received as patients by the Sanitarium, 438 were born in Russia, and 305 in the United States (presumably of Russian parentage, largely). England, Austro-Hungary, Germany and Roumania had each from 11 to 20 representatives.

As a third form of its activity, the society sends many excursionists to Rockaway Park by train. An opportunity is afforded for ocean bathing. That the Hebrew Sanitarium treats its wards with great liberality will appear from this extract from one of its recent reports: "Car fare, ferry tickets, and railroad transportation are furnished free to all attending the excursions—thus no poor person can say they cannot afford to avail themselves of the benefits offered by our Society."

---

[1] Fifteenth Annual Report, 1893, p. 36. In the absence of more detailed statistics this figure is made the basis for estimating total beneficiaries previous to 1892.

The organization each summer maintains a down-town office within the general area from which its beneficiaries are drawn. Any adult may here apply for tickets to the train or boat excursions. Experience has taught the society that it is necessary to guard against giving tickets directly to children. Instances are cited where tickets thus obtained have been sold. An adult is at liberty to apply as often as he likes during the season. There is no desire to restrict beneficiaries to a single excursion. Those who have gone by boat may next time go by train, and *vice versa*. When one remembers that the children of Hebrew parentage are by no means restricted to this charity which particularly singles them out, but that the hospitality of several other Fresh Air agencies in the city is at their command, one better appreciates the generous scale on which the philanthropy operates in their behalf.

Tribune Fresh Air Fund.—The origin of this work has been briefly told.[1] It is impossible to refrain from reprinting a letter written at the time the movement was launched. Its enthusiasm is still contagious.

"Sherman, Penn., June 3, 1877.
My Dear Mrs. L.—The ball is set in motion. I took for my text this morning, 'Inasmuch as ye have done it unto one of the least of these, ye have done it unto me,' and made the practical bearing of my words the bringing out into our homes some of the waifs and outcasts of the city. One man stopped on his way home to say that he would take four. In another house there is a call for a mother and baby, and so on through the town. The enthusiasm and response of my people have delighted me. Next to get the money, then to tell the children. Must not two weeks in this pure mountain air be felt by them in after life? It seems to me that they are all but here! . . . I shall try for a pass over the road to go back and forth with the children myself, and perhaps I can arrange with some of the good people on the way, to bring us a country lunch as the train comes along. Some good angel whisper it in the ear of a little one! Tell a tired mother there is life for her child in this country air! WILLARD PARSONS."[2]

The railroad gave the pass and half-fare rates for the children. Postal cards dropped *en route* described the experience of the first expedition.

"Ridgewood.—No more trouble with lunch bundles. Lunches nearly

[1] p. 18.
[2] "One Summer's Work." Eleanor I. Lovett. *Sunday Afternoon* Vol. I., pp. 423-432.

used up. One eye treated for cinders. Train boy has asked if these are all my family!"

"Turner's.—One towel and handkerchief needed. One girl sick. My youngest asleep. The E. boys eat all the time. More eyes treated with success at Monroe."

Any one who has ever helped to get Fresh Air children to their destination in the country will appreciate this description.

The policy here inaugurated of securing free entertainment in the country for children of the tenements has been adhered to, from that day to this. Other features, such as the day excursion and the colonization of children in Summer Homes have been added to the original plan. But unlike many country week societies, the Tribune never pays board to private families.

In the past, the Tribune Fund has contributed to the support of Fresh Air work in no less than five directions: (1) Transportation expenses of those sent to private families by other societies or by individuals; (2) transportation expenses of those sent to Homes supported by other local societies—missions, college settlements and the like; (3) transportation expenses of its own beneficiaries sent to Homes under its own care; (4) transportation expenses of its own beneficiaries sent as guests to private families inviting children through the Tribune Fresh Air Fund; (5) operating expenses of Homes supported by the Fund.

In former years, the number of those sent out under the first two provisions was by no means small, reaching in one year a total of a thousand children, exclusive of "Life's" beneficiaries.[1] But in 1895, subsidies of this sort were almost entirely withheld, owing to a decrease in the amount at the disposal of the Tribune for its own wards. The same year, the Fund had at its disposal twelve Fresh Air Homes to which it sent no fewer than 3,000 children. The Tribune Fund was called upon to pay the running expenses of but two of these Homes—the Ashford Hill Retreat, at Ardsley, N. Y., and Eunice Home, at Chapel Hill, N. J. These two Homes accommodated about as many as the other ten, or 1,574 children. 65 per cent. of the Fund went for traveling expenses of children and attendants. Even were the proportion greater, it would be a mistake to regard the Tribune Fresh Air Fund as solely a transportation agency. Naturally those accustomed in other years to look to the Fund to provide tickets for their wards might so consider it. But its main business has not been to subsidize the work of other societies.

[1] See p. 55.

Mr. Parsons has called attention to three factors in the work.[1] These are, (1) money; (2) homes; (3) children. As for the first, we are told that two or three appeals in the course of the season to the Fund's constituency are usually sufficient to call out the contributions needed. It is not so simple a matter to secure places of entertainment. General appeals are useless. Letters, circular or personal, are not much better. It is necessary to visit the towns to which it is desired to send the children, to call upon the clergy and influential citizens of the place; to interest the editor of the local paper; perhaps to arrange for a public meeting; at any rate, to see that a responsible committee is appointed to canvass the locality. This preliminary work must largely be repeated each year. The task long since outgrew Mr. Parsons' ability to conduct in person the entire campaign. Reliance must now be had upon the assistance of others.

In the selection of children, coöperation is assured. Application from workers among the poor, from missionaries, teachers, nurses, settlement residents and others are filed with the Fund. Mr. Parsons has had the assistance of nearly 200 such workers in a single year.

Statistics are at best but a poor medium for conveying an adequate idea of the amount of time and nervous energy contributed by those who gather up the children. When these have been found —not in itself a difficult task—they are to be examined by a physician to guard against the presence of two dreaded foes of the work: contagious disease and vermin. If the first has slain the hopes of thousands, the last has destroyed the chances of tens of thousands. In a single year, out of 15,000 children examined, about one-third passed muster. Doubtless the fact that the children are received as guests, makes insistence upon clean heads the more essential. It is this work of preparing the children for the country, that falls upon the workers among the poor.

Then again, it is no easy matter to fit the right children into the right families. Questions of religious faith and of nationality have to be considered. Catholic children of Italian parentage and the children of orthodox Jews are by no means easily placed in private homes. Matters of cleanliness and of dietary laws enter in to complicate the situation. Families in the country, too, frequently experience a kind of shock, induced by the very neatness and respect-

---

[1] "Story of the Fresh Air Fund," Willard Parsons. Scribner's Magazine, Vol. IX., No. 4, April, 1891.

ability of the children sent to them. Sensational newspaper accounts of cases of dire poverty in city slums, often become the basis for picturing how the Fresh Air child ought to look.

That amid these and other difficulties, Mr. Parsons has continued to emphasize the principle of free entertainment, speaks well for the practicability of the method when backed by personal enthusiasm and effort. What widespread interest this form of Fresh Air work has awakened is a matter of record. Committees from Toronto, Montreal, St. Johns, London and Manchester have visited New York to study its methods. Germany, Italy and even Russia have sent for information, while "Dresden, Stuttgart, Vienna, and Berlin have each joined the movement." Meantime the influence of Mr. Parsons' work at home cannot be estimated.

It can scarcely be thought ungracious, after that which has been said, to indicate what, from the statistician's point of view, must seem defects or at least limitations in the charity. The very method of providing for the executive expenses of the Fund, seems one of these limitations.[1]

In the desire not to use a penny of contributions for defraying expenses of registration, office room and the like, there is a probability that the value of systematic records will be underestimated. Thus, for example, for lack of office space and a clerical force to do the work, no list of the names with addresses of beneficiaries is kept at headquarters. Reliance is placed upon the judgment and discretion of the individual worker. If the same child is invited by name to revisit its host the following year, the agencies which chanced to send children through the Tribune on the particular date on which a party of children were sent to the town in question, must be consulted for the purpose of finding the child wanted. The Fund concerns itself chiefly with the total number of children sent out on a given date by a particular society or individual.

Is such economy in executive management a real virtue? How valuable, if only for purposes of comparison, an alphabetical registration of beneficiaries with their addresses and the name of the agency recommending them, would have been. That some such record was not deemed impracticable is shown by the offer of the Charity Organization Society to keep such a list in the interest of discriminate relief-giving. Records of this kind on the part of the Tribune Fund would have shown, when compared, all duplications

[1] A few wealthy gentlemen meet all the expenses of management.

among beneficiaries; how far the same children were sent year after year; how the work was distributed among various agencies and in particular sections of the city; and indirectly, the presence of favoritism or lack of discrimination on the part of the children's champions. If other societies had also been led by the Tribune's example to keep systematic records, much overlapping and probable "overlooking" might have been saved. The interests of economy as well as of scientific charity, would have warranted expenditure to this end. In short, such registration would have enabled the Fund to reduce to a minimum the abuses likely to arise where charity is dealt out without systematic record of its beneficiaries. Even workers among the poor, in their enthusiasm for their own charges, are not always impartial judges of where the greatest need is for the distribution of Fresh Air privileges.

Mr. Parsons seems to have questioned whether his work might not be strengthened in some of these respects. He says: "Perhaps the time is near at hand when the work should be more systematically developed. I am quite certain that a large number of skilled and paid helpers could be employed with most satisfactory results." This, however, was written five years ago and still awaits accomplishment. As agencies multiply and Fresh Air work grows more complex the need of discrimination in the selection of its beneficiaries becomes the more imperative.

In addition to its country week work, the Tribune Fresh Air Fund conducts day excursions for mothers and children. One gentleman meets the entire expense of these outings.

All Souls' (P. E.) Church.—Two things stand out conspicuously in the Fresh Air relief work of this church. One of these is that, although the charity is supported largely from within the parish, it may fairly claim to belong to the non-sectarian societies. All Souls' Summer Home, at Sea Cliff, Long Island, receives children, irrespective of creed or nationality. Hebrews and Roman Catholics as well as Protestants are welcomed. The caretakers are from various denominations. Thus the work of All Souls' is almost unique in ecclesiastical Fresh Air annals.[1] Such a "losing of

---

[1] A second instance, somewhat similar, is the work of the Men's Guild of St. Luke's Church, Scranton. For an example of a different spirit, compare the following: "Our Fresh Air work is used as a kind of reward for attendance at our missions. Many Roman Catholics are in our sewing schools, where they learn verses of scripture. Some of these children are taken to the Home in hopes of teaching them 'the better way.'" (Interview with Fresh Air worker of a Church Home.)

one's self" is refreshing to contemplate. The simplicity of the religious services at Sea Cliff makes it possible for the children of different faiths to participate.

A second characteristic of the charity is its adoption, from the first, of the cottage system. The Home will accommodate 100 children. These are distributed in seven cottages, the largest, capable of receiving 20, the smaller ones, 14 or 15 children. The houses have small rooms, containing from one to four beds. In charge of each cottage is a housemother. The president of the Home, writes: "These caretakers volunteer their services, they are young women of refinement and education, and their influence over the children is very great. We try in every case to select those who need the outing quite as much as the children, but always those who are specially adapted to this work for Christ and His little ones."

It is to be said that the close proximity of the cottages, and the fact that they are chiefly sleeping quarters—the children mingling at play and at meals—makes the family units somewhat more theoretical than real. Then also, the houses are of two stories and cut up into small rooms. This makes it more difficult for the housemothers to keep watch over their protégés, and also adds to the cost of repairs, cleaning and the like. At the same time, such cottages make possible nicer age and sex classification—no small advantage. Undoubtedly, too, they help to make more personal the work of each caretaker and to give a more homelike atmosphere to the philanthropy. The effort here made is to avoid the evils of colonization while reaping its advantages.

All Souls' work is by no means a cheap charity. The records show that it costs to give a child a two weeks' outing, nearly ten dollars, notwithstanding the fact that the housemothers receive only their living expenses, while the salaries paid to matron and superintendent are but nominal. Transportation is also inexpensive. Probably the cottage system as here carried out is more or less responsible for the high per capita cost. Although the parish might do its work more cheaply than it does, one cannot say that any considerable retrenchment of expense would be either wise or possible under the circumstances.

The ease of access to the Home from the city, has enabled parents to visit their offspring on Sundays. Experience proves that the custom is a bad one, demoralizing alike to parents and children. The latter are often made homesick by the sight of their own people, while not infrequently the visitors expect the Home authorities to provide dinners and even return tickets. The Sunday afternoon talks by the housemothers to their little families—talks on such practical subjects as cleanliness, obedience and the like—are seriously interrupted by such visits and the educational influence of the Home to this extent impaired.

The experience on this point is not peculiar to All Souls'. Except in case of serious illness, parents and friends should not visit the children during the outing.

The Bartholdi Crèche.—Notwithstanding the many forms of Fresh Air relief, it was felt that there was need of another type of the charity to fill a want still left unmet. In 1886, the Bartholdi Crèche was organized, "to meet the needs of poor mothers and children *who cannot leave their homes to stay over night, or even a whole day*, at any of the more distant fresh air resorts, and to whom the opportunity of spending a few hours amid green fields and in pure air is an inestimable remedial boon. A mother can take her sick babe at a moment's notice, and reach at once bracing air and shady groves, when the delay necessary to gain a more distant point might be fatal." To this end, privileges of Bedloe's, Ward's and Randall's Island have been successively extended to the Crèche by the proper authorities in each case.

The statistics of what the Crèche has accomplished in the last ten years, together with the fact that this Fresh Air agency, in the summer of 1896, finds its island privileges withdrawn, serve to emphasize the need of easier access for the tenement-house population in summer to the salt-water breezes of New York harbor. With its splendid island facilities given over to public institutions, rare opportunities for Fresh Air relief are lost to Greater New York, and the necessity for charity, always a mixed blessing, involving moral peril both to him who gives and to him who receives, is thereby augmented.[1]

This latter danger, the managers of the Crèche have attempted to reduce to a minimum. Only children liable to disease are received with their caretakers. The beneficiaries, as a rule, pay their own car fares. Medical attendance is provided. The medical director testifies that the lives of many children have been saved by the timely

---

[1] The recent decision to build one or more Fresh Air resorts above the docks will afford not a little relief to the tenement district.

use of the hospitalities of the Crèche. The average per capita cost of the work in 1895 was 10.6 cents. The ratio of mothers to infants and children under twelve is 1 to 2.

Life's Fresh Air Fund.—One of the striking illustrations of the debt of Fresh Air charity to the press is the persistent and successful efforts of "Life." For almost a decade, this weekly has undertaken to secure the wherewithal to send poor children to the country for a fortnight's vacation. In number of days' outings provided, it stands fourth in our list of the general Fresh Air societies of the city.

For two years, the Fund maintained what it called "Life's Village," at Eatontown, N. J. The settlement consisted of cottages, each presided over by a housemother. In 1891, an estate of fourteen acres was leased at Branchville, in the town of Ridgefield, Conn. Here "Life's Farm" was established. About 1,150 children are entertained at Branchville in the season. Up to 1894, Life also boarded in the country hundreds of children whom it could not accommodate at its own Home.

The management of the Fund is in the same hands as that of the Tribune. In fact Mr. Parsons provides free transportation for Life's beneficiaries, from the Tribune Fresh Air Fund. This is to be remembered when we come to consider the total number of beneficiaries of the general Fresh Air Charities and also the cost per capita to the different agencies.

The New York Association for Improving the Condition of the Poor.—For several years previous to 1890, the N. Y. A. I. C. P. had done considerable Fresh Air work through other agencies, such as the Children's Aid Society and the Tribune Fund. In the annual report for 1888, the hope is expressed that the Association may at no distant day have a Summer Home of its own. Two years later, its "Ocean Parties" were inaugurated "to provide pure air, sea bathing and wholesome food for the laboring poor who are compelled to live in stuffy tenement houses and who cannot afford to pay for such recreation." Among the rules for the management of these excursions is the following: "No beneficiaries shall receive tickets for these parties until their circumstances shall have been first carefully and personally investigated by the visitors of the Association under the direction of the General Agent."

The absolute necessity of such precaution is evident from the character of the outings. Use is made of the regular steamers plying between the city and Coney Island. The parties are tri-weekly. The Association's wards are allowed the freedom of the boat and are scarcely to be distinguished from other excursionists. Arriving at Coney Island, after the long sail down the bay, the society's guests are marshalled for the short railway journey to the Home of the Association. Here a substantial meal welcomes the visitors upon their arrival. Bathing follows at a safe interval. The younger children find special delight in the sand. This part of the work is distinctly recreational. There is another side, however, which emphasizes the recuperative purpose of the Association's Fresh Air relief.

At its People's Seaside Home, beginning with 1892, provision was made for the reception of cripples, convalescents or aged people, who were entertained for periods ranging from one to four weeks. In 1893, a building to be known as the "Free Home for Ailing and Crippled Children," was set apart for the use of children of country week age, say from six to twelve or fourteen years old. When accompanied by older brothers or sisters, children younger than six are sometimes received. An administration cottage separates the children's quarters from the building now occupied by aged women, together with mothers and their babies. This provision for the retention of its wards for days or weeks may be considered the recuperative side of the work.

The Association has gone one step farther. It is now engaged in an attempt to combine *recreation* and *education.* The society provides teachers for the children and mothers who are its guests for a fortnight. A kindergartner, an instructress in nature studies, and a cooking teacher organized classes this past summer. Girls, and mothers, too, have been taught not only how to prepare dishes but how to market. So far from detracting from the value or interest of the vacation, the teachers report that these features have given an added zest to the outing.

This is hardly the place to call attention to another departure in the summer work of this society, as seen in its Vacation Schools, where in the densely crowded districts of the city, children of the tenements are taken off the streets for a few hours each day and taught many useful lessons by the methods of "organized play." Whatever one may think of the wisdom of offering as a charity "free recreation" to the poor, the giving of free education safeguards its own distribution. The Vacation School is a happy combination of recreation and education at the door of the tenements.

It should be said, finally, that while few Fresh Air societies are more liberal in their treatment of their wards, few have better facilities for seeking out worthy cases. Through its constant relations with "the other half" and by means of its corps of trained visitors, it is able to protect itself against much of the imposition that its liberality would otherwise invite. Alphabetical lists of its beneficiaries are kept as an additional safeguard.

The George Junior Republic.[1]—A small volume might be written about this one experiment in Fresh Air charity. The movement is unique in the history of Fresh Air endeavor. A few of the characteristic features of the Republic may be noted in the course of its evolution. So much has recently been written upon the subject that the more conspicuous traits of the work are well known.[2] Mr. George began by taking a few children from mission schools in the city, to Freeville, N. Y., where they were given two weeks of country life. The churches of the region were asked to contribute food and clothing for the support of the Camp. The dangers of promiscuous Fresh Air work soon appeared. Mr. George found that many of the children were sent to the country for the sake of the spoils. Impositions practiced upon him on two successive winters by families of his Fresh Air children convinced him of the danger of giving something for nothing. On the other hand, the difficulty of properly protecting the property of his neighbors from the raids of his wards, emphasized the need of vigorous discipline. In a single day, Mr. George had occasion to thrash 32 boys for stealing apples. He declares it to have been the meanest day's work that he ever did. How to secure effective discipline, how to escape pauperizing his beneficiaries, these were the two problems which his experience had set him. The Junior Republic, as now organized, is the result of the attempt to solve both problems.

For the first time in the conduct of either charitable or correctional work, so far as known, two principles, fundamental to our

[1] The description here given is based upon a personal visit to the Republic in the summer of 1896, and the interviews held with Mr. George at that time.

[2] Probably no Fresh Air enterprise ever received so much newspaper notoriety, some of which could not have been altogether agreeable to its founder and early patrons. Since this sentence was written, word comes that the trustees of the Republic have distinctly repudiated certain methods adopted by a metropolitan daily to "benefit" the philanthropy.

present social order were made the essential characteristics of the Republic. These two principles are self-government and self-help. Courts of justice and the machinery of popular elections were set up. Mr. George became, temporarily, president of the Republic with right of absolute veto. A Senate and House of Representatives legislated upon matters pertaining to the government of the colony. Offices in the civil service were filled from a list of candidates who had succeeded in passing satisfactory examinations. A police force acted as the executive arm of the government. Trial by jury extended to any citizen accused of crime a chance to be judged by his peers. Mr. George sought, in this way, to remove from the minds of his wards any sense of arbitrary authority on his part and at the same time to acquaint them with the forms of government under which their lives were to be spent.

A similar educational purpose is apparent in the adoption of the economic principle of self-help. To teach the boys and girls that they need never expect to receive something for nothing in the real work-a-day world, became one of the chief aims of the Republic. A system of currency was adopted. Workshops were established which, with the farm and domestic requirements of the colony, created abundant demand for labor. Everything received—food, clothing, shelter, must be paid for from the earnings of industry. If any would not work neither should he eat. An almshouse and a jail were provided for social dependents and delinquents.

While the compelling impulse toward this work had been distinctly religious, practical difficulties had led Mr. George to make his appeal to the entire range of motives that obtain in real life. The self-interest of the citizen, his ambition, pride and desire to get on, were given a normal place in the social scheme. The Republic's president recognized that in a democracy, church and state must be separate; that religion is an individual matter. Attendance upon Sunday school, prayer meetings and preaching services became voluntary. A group of Christians among the children were encouraged to talk with their comrades and to secure their presence at these meetings so far as possible, but persuasion became the sole instrument employed in religious work.

Three conditions upon which Mr. George lays stress differentiate this form of Fresh Air charity from that of other agencies. These are: (1) The age of the children received. Fresh Air philanthropy, ordinarily, makes no provision for older boys. The large boy is considered an element of danger to any well-ordered and decorous Fresh Air charity. The Republic receives both boys and girls between the ages of twelve and seventeen.[1]

(2) The character of the children. Fresh Air charities usually have, at least, a minimum standard of moral excellence for their beneficiaries. It would be nearer the truth to say that Mr. George has a standard of moral badness. Certainly the tougher the boy is, the better seems his chance of admission to the young commonwealth. The street idler, the leader of the "gang," the bully who is the terror of his neighborhood, the boy who is unmanageable at home, these are the types on whose reformation the Republic stakes its reputation. Nor does Mr. George hesitate about admitting girls to the privileges of the Camp. Girls are to be found in the homes of the boys; the sexes mingle at their work or at play. Why should artificial conditions be created to save boys and girls from a contact as inevitable as nature's own laws? If one may judge from the appearance of the girls, as well as from the jail and almshouse records of the Camp, the girls are, on the whole, of a higher moral grade than the boys. Their influence would seem to make for law and order in the Republic.

(3) Length of time for which the beneficiaries are received. Mr. George began his Fresh Air work by taking children to the country for a fortnight each summer. As the educational side of the charity developed, he found two months the shortest possible time in which to impress the lessons of the vacation upon the minds and hearts of his wards.

It will be clear from these considerations, that the work at Freeville has a different scope from the Fresh Air charity of regulation type. The aim of the Republic is quite as much moral as physical restoration. Since moral degeneracy may be the cause as well as the effect of physical debility, New York is to be congratulated that two months of country life have been provided for the class from which dependents and delinquents are but too often recruited. Should this work develop ultimately, as it now promises to do, into a permanent training school for moral convalescents, and thus cease to be distinctively a summer charity, the George Junior Republic will none the less redound to the credit of the Fresh Air movement.

---

[1] Unfortunately, this rule is not strictly adhered to. For a sympathetic account of the Republic, together with friendly criticism of some of its limitations, see article by Washington Gladden in "The Outlook," October 31, 1896.

Little Mothers' Aid Association. —Infants in arms, young children, even the street tough have been provided for. What shall be said of the "little mother," the girl from seven to fourteen, whose lot compels her to care for younger brothers and sisters as if they were her own offspring? She cannot well be spared to go to the country with her more fortunate mates. The society named in her honor comes to her relief. Through the Little Mothers' Aid Association, she may be taken out to one of the city's suburban parks, situated on Long Island Sound. There the authorities have loaned a house for use from June to October. Three lines of conveyance, at a considerable expense of both time and money must be taken to reach Pelham Bay Park. Once there, the combined elements of a country and seashore picnic are to be had. Both breakfast and dinner are served to the little mothers. A doctor is in attendance who examines them before they take their dip in the Sound. The ones who need it most are invited to spend a few days at the holiday house in the Park.

The Association selects its wards through "chaperons" who are employed to visit the crowded tenement districts of the city in search of little mothers. The chaperons are expected to devote one day of each week to selecting their protégées, one day to the outing, and half a day in visiting cases of special need. Lessons in cooking, mending and general housework are provided for those who visit at the holiday house.

Summer Shelter of Morristown. —This society is the outgrowth of the "Wednesday Afternoon Sewing Class of Morristown." Two articles of the constitution account for the place here given the Shelter among the general Fresh Air charities of New York City. According to this constitution (Art. II.), "the object of the 'Summer Shelter' is to receive, during summer months, poor children, from New York City, requiring country air." And, again (Art. XII.), "'The Summer Shelter' shall be non-sectarian in all its work." In 1895, among the charities of New York City that availed themselves of the coöperation of the Shelter were the Charity Organization Society, The Tenement House District of King's Daughters, Sunnyside Nursery, Little Mothers' Aid Association and East Side House. Special cases were received from Brooklyn and Jersey City. Each member of the visiting committee, acting in turn, oversees the Home for one week and reports its condition to the president. Marked importance is attached to the position of matron, and the qualifications for the office "embody all that is highest and best in woman."

Gilbert A. Robertson Home.—This philanthropy has one feature which places it in a class by itself. The Gilbert A. Robertson Home treats the family as a unit. Few Fresh Air societies make any provision for working men. This one welcomes the man with his wife and children. Mr. Robertson's widow left property valued at more than $120,000, to found, in memory of her husband, a home for the worthy poor, where they could enjoy all the privileges of a hotel.[1] A visit to the Home at Scarsdale, N. Y., will convince one that the trustees of the fund have provided such a "hotel." The location is commanding. A mansion of twenty-two rooms, to which fifteen have since been added, and eighteen acres of ground afford ample provision for fifty or sixty guests. Separate apartments are assigned each family. The women take care of their own rooms. There are two adjoining dining-rooms, one for the parents, another for the children and mothers with infants. A playroom for the children and living rooms for the adults add to the comfort. The guests are at liberty to go and come at will, provided that they are promptly on hand at their meals and at bedtime. The farm supplies the table with milk, eggs and fresh vegetables. It is not surprising that more than 500 families should apply at the city office for entertainment during the summer.

An interesting question arises as to how far the Home is actually reaching the heads of families. Excellent statistics are furnished us. An analysis of them from the beginning of the work in 1891, gives this table:

Year.	Families Represented.	Number of Men.	Percentage of Men.	Percentage of Women.	Percentage of Children.
1891	...	8	5.8	33.5	60.5
1892	105	22	6.6	31.4	61.9
1893	146	25	5.4	30.4	64.1
1894	153	38	7.7	29.9	62.2
1895	140	55	11.3	25.3	63.3

Of the 55 men reported for 1895, three or four were the older sons of widows and the chief support of the family. Generally, the term men signifies the father of the family. There would appear from these figures to be a steady increase in the percentage of men.

[1] Report of the G. A. R. Home, 1892.

As the number of applications increases, it becomes easier to select families, where, other things being equal, the father is at liberty to enjoy the outing with his family. Another principle of selection is that the same family shall not be entertained for more than three seasons in succession.

Lana ac Tela Society.—The same impulse that led a few children to dress dolls and send them to poor little girls in the hospital, led these same children, now grown to womanhood, to organize a society whose chief end should be to provide children and mothers with a country holiday. A characteristic of the work, as one might expect from the circumstances of its origin, is the amount of personal attention which the charity has received from its projectors. Girls, women, and mothers with their babies are admitted to the privileges of the Home at Nyack. Great pains are taken to give a family atmosphere to the place. The dormitory system is eschewed. Four beds in a room is the largest number allowed. Many of the summer residents of Nyack throw open their private grounds for the enjoyment of the society's guests. The Nyack Steamboat Company also extends the freedom of its ferry to them. Many hours are frequently spent on the upper deck of the "Rockland" as she plies across the Hudson. River wading furnishes a safe substitute for bathing.[1]

Christian Herald Children's Home.—The most recent as well as one of the most enthusiastic of the general Fresh Air charities on our list is the Christian Herald Children's Home. Mr. Klopsch, the proprietor of the religious journal from which the Home is named, personally superintends the conduct of the philanthropy. He appeals for financial assistance to the readers of the Herald. Accommodations are had for 250 children. The field of selection is various missions in New York. While Roman Catholics and Hebrews are received, the usual method of invitation is such that Protestant children are the chief ones to apply. "The poorer they are the better we like it," says Mr. Klopsch. The work opens in June with children who are too ill to attend school. Much is made of religious and patriotic exercises. One caretaker or "missionary" is provided for every fifteen or twenty wards.

---

[1] The Home was rented for 1896 to another society for vacation purposes.

I.—GENERAL OR NON-SECTARIAN FRESH AIR SOCIETIES OF NEW YORK CITY.

The description which has been given of the fourteen Fresh Air agencies here enumerated, will serve to justify their classification under the head of "General or Non-Sectarian." An exception might be taken in the case of the Sanitarium for Hebrew Children which is designed for those of Jewish faith. Since, however, neither national nor congregational lines are observed in the administration of the relief, but Russian and English, orthodox and liberal Jews are treated alike, it is sufficiently accurate to include the Sanitarium with the others.

It is possible in the case of these general and local charities to present statistics covering the full term of their activities. The data relating to the individual societies may be summarized in comprehensive totals.

TABLE I.—GENERAL STATISTICS.

	Society.	Date.	No. Sent for One Day.	No. Sent for more than One Day.	Average Days' Stay.	Total Beneficiaries.	Total Days' Outings.
1	St. J. G.	1874	652,760	13,973 av.	8+	666,733	760,152
2	C. A. S.	1874	67,792	84,910	6	152,702	577,252
3	San. H. C.	1877	170,869	2,172	8 e	173,041	188,245
4	Tribune	1877	165,335[1]	141,284[2]	14	306,619	2,143,311[3]
5	All Souls'	1882	......	6,600	14 a	6,600	92,400
6	Barth. Cr.	1886	48,757	......	..	48,757	48,757
7	Life	1887	......	17,524	14[4]	17,524	245,336
8	A. I. C. P.	1890	112,287	1,633	11 a	113,920	130,250
9	Jr. Rep.	1890		1,196 / 147	14 / 60	1,343	25,564
10	L. M. A.	1890	7,478	275	3	7,753	8,303
11	S. S. M.	1890	......	950	14	950	13,300
12	G. A. R. H.	1891	......	1,901	12+	1,901	22,832
13	L. a. T. S.	1892	......	1,000 a	14	1,000 a	14,000
14	C. H. C. H.	1894	......	3,578	10	3,578	35,780
	Totals		1,225,278	277,143	11	1,502,421	4,311,482
	Total Duplications		......	19,560		19,560	273,840
	Revised Totals		1,225,278	257,583		1,482,861	4,037,642

[1] 60,000 were from Brooklyn.
[2] 12,000 were from Brooklyn.
[3] 228,000 days' outings given to Brooklyn beneficiaries.
[4] For 1887-1889 the number of beneficiaries is given only approximately.
   a Approximate.   e Estimated.

To economize space and time in printing the tables these abbreviated forms of the societies' names are employed. The key is given once for all.

1 St. J. G.—St. John's Guild.
2 C. A. S.—Children's Aid Society.
3 San. H. C.—Sanitarium for Hebrew Children.
4 Tribune.—Tribune Fresh Air Fund.
5 All Souls'.—All Souls' P. E. Church.
6 Barth. Cr.—Bartholdi Crèche.
7 Life.—Life Fresh Air Fund.
8 A. I. C. P.—Association for Improving the Condition of the Poor.
9 Jr. Rep.—George Junior Republic.
10 L. M. A.—Little Mothers' Aid Association.
11 S. S. M.—Summer Shelter of Morristown.
12 G. A. R. H.—Gilbert A. Robertson Home.
13 L. a. T. S.—Lana ac Tela Society.
14 C. H. C. H.—Christian Herald Children's Home.

An analysis of the data of Table I. discovers three striking examples of duplication of record, and one instance of triplication. The manifold character of Mr. Parsons' Tribune work has been pointed out. Where the Tribune has furnished transportation to the wards of the other Fresh Air societies enumerated, there is sure to be a duplication of counting in the records, since each agency places such beneficiaries to its own credit in making up its totals. The Tribune always provides transportation for the children whom Life entertains in the country. Until 1895, the Tribune did the same thing for the wards of the George Junior Republic and the Lana ac Tela Society. Here are children counted twice in three cases. One instance of triplication comes about in this way. In its account of its work for 1893, Life mentions that it sent 120 children to Freeville. These beneficiaries were undoubtedly sent to Mr. George, who counted them in the census of his summer camp. The Tribune paid their fare and therefore also counted them. The 120 children have now trebled and the 360 children resulting are each credited with 14 days in the country. The total of such duplications in Table I. amounts to 19,560 cases credited with 273,840 extra days' outings. Our first summary must be revised to that extent. Having eliminated, as far as discoverable, all instances of duplication, we are prepared to discuss intelligently the general results of nonsectarian Fresh Air philanthropy in New York City.

Of the total number of beneficiaries, 1,225,278, or 82.6 per cent., were day excursionists. 257,583, or 17 per cent., were given vacations ranging from 3 days to 60 days. It is worth while to note that although the "country-weekers" were so small a proportion of the total beneficiaries, yet they received the larger share of days' outings. Of the 4,037,642 holidays given in all, 2,812,364 of them, or 69 per cent. were enjoyed by the country-weekers, who, as we just saw, were but 17 per cent. of the whole number of beneficiaries. Their average vacation was 10.9 days.

Of the 14 societies of Table I., 6 engage in both types of Fresh Air charity. The relative disproportion in the number of days' outings devoted by each society to one or the other form of relief, is sufficiently large to enable us to determine at once to which of the two classes, the agency in question the more properly belongs. For instance, with 652,760 out of 766,152 days' outings, given by its Floating Hospital, St. John's Guild clearly emphasizes the day excursion. On the other hand, the Tribune Fresh Air Fund, while actually reporting a larger number sent away for the day than for a fortnight, should be classified with country week societies. The 46 per cent. of its wards who were country-weekers received 92 per cent. of all the holidays reported by the Fund. The 7 societies which engage in country week work only, are, for the most part, the smaller and younger of the organizations enumerated.

One can hardly have failed to observe that the total days' outings are distributed very unevenly among these 14 societies. One agency is credited with quite half of all the holidays given. 50 per cent. of the societies furnished 95 per cent. of the days' outings.

Of course, the same individual may be sent away by the same society year after year. In the case of the day excursions, the child and its caretaker may attend several times in a season. Therefore the 1,482,861 beneficiaries reported as the result of these years of Fresh Air work, are by no means so many distinct individuals. One case comes to mind where a woman, twenty-four years old, the mother of eight children, had been received annually, bringing not only her youngest born to the sanatorium, but the major part of her family.

We may be sure that the total volume of Fresh Air work done by New York agencies since the New York Times gave its first excursions in 1872, is not exaggerated in the summaries here given. For it is to be kept in mind that we are dealing now only with the general societies. In addition to their activity is that of the various churches and other parochial organizations doing an independent work. 18 such agencies report over 100,000 days' outings, as compared with less than 400,000 given the same year by the non-sectarian agencies. We are fully warranted in concluding that the totals presented in Table I., are distinctly conservative—especially if taken to represent the total volume of Fresh Air work of the city between 1874 and 1895 inclusive.

What story do these figures tell? Graphically they show that within a quarter of a century a philanthropy has grown up which has transported a million and a half of people, chiefly women and children, to the seashore or the country, and given to each one nearly three days' vacation. An equivalent of this would be the giving of a day's outing by private charity to nearly every man, woman and child in London, or to one out of every 15 persons in the United States at the last census. It is as if each inhabitant of the New York of 1890, had received 2.6 days' outings at the hands of some one of these 14 societies.

Excursionists and Visitors.

Coming now to the statistics of these fourteen General Societies for a single year, 1895, their beneficiaries may be distributed into the two classes shown in Table II.

TABLE II.—EXCURSIONISTS AND VISITORS IN 1895.

	Society.	Day Excursionists.	Visitors.	Average Days' Stay.	Total Days' Outing.
1	St. J. G.	56,063	1,643	8[1]	69,411
2	C. A. S.	5,326	6,599	6	44,920
3	San. H. C.	13,392	803	8[e]	19,816
4	Tribune	28,924[2]	6,841	14	124,698
5	All Souls'		50	7	
			550	14	8,050
6	Barth. Cr.	11,767			11,767
7	Life		1,180	14	16,520
8	A. I. C. P.	19,576	601	11[3]	26,232
9	Jr. Rep.		147	60	8,820
10	L. M. A.	1,242	83	3[e]	1,491
11	S. S. M.		180	14	2,520
12	G. A. R. H.		485	12[4]	5,847
13	L.a. T. S.		280	14	3,920
14	C. H. C. H.		2,378	10	23,780
	Total	136,290	21,820	10.6	367,792

[1] Where the "average days' stay" of the "visitors" is given approximately, as in this case, and in that of the Sanitarium for Hebrew Children and of the Robertson Home, the exact total days' outings furnished the visitors is indicated below. Here the exact total is 13,348 days.
[2] Cf. notes, Table I.
[3] Exact total, 6,656 days.
[4] Exact total, 5,847⅔ days.

Of the 158,110 total beneficiaries, 136,290, or 86 per cent., were day excursionists; and 21,820, or 13.8 per cent., were "country-weekers," that is, visitors. The 86 per cent. of excursionists enjoyed but 37 per cent. of the total days' outings, while the nearly 14 per cent. who were visitors, enjoyed 63 per cent. of the holidays. The average length of vacation for the beneficiaries as a whole was 2½ days; and for the country-weekers alone, 10⅔ days. We may need to remind ourselves once more, that the 136,290 excursionists were not so many individuals. Probably each excursionist was in attendance, on the average, two or three times in a season. Since duplications are not noted in the records of any of the societies, the only basis for such a conjecture is, of course, the estimates of the officers of the various societies, as to what is true of their own work.

The argument in favor of such duplication is apparent. Since the very *raison d' être* of the excursions is to furnish fresh air to those who cannot go to the country or be sent away to stay over night, why should not such be given sufficient day trips to compensate for the deprivation? 40,000 to 50,000 would perhaps be a conservative estimate of the number of separate individuals who made up the 136,290 attendances on excursions during the season.

Adults and Children.

There are two general age classes into which Fresh Air societies divide their beneficiaries. These are "adults" and "children." Duplication of records in 1895 was reduced to a minimum. The only one of our general societies assisted by the Tribune Fund that year was Life, whose wards are always furnished transportation by Mr. Parsons. Account of this fact is taken in the tabulation by subtracting Life's 1,180 beneficiaries from the Tribune's total.

We have previously noted how generally the philanthropy has sustained its original character as a children's charity. Disregarding the Tribune excursions, whose beneficiaries are unclassified, the proportion of adults to children is 28.9 per cent. Three-fourths of the adults are reported by societies which receive the caretaker for the child's sake. The ratio of adults to children also throws light upon the conditions of admission to a society's privileges. The adults of St. John's Guild were 36 per cent. of the total beneficiaries, that is, there was one caretaker to less than two children. In the case of the Hebrew Sanitarium the adults were 27 per cent. of the whole, or one caretaker to almost three children. The difference is to be accounted for from the fact that the Guild centers its activity upon sick babies and young children, while the Sanitarium does not make illness a condition, nor is its age limit so low. The N. Y. A. I. C. P., in 1895, sent 31 per cent. of adults. Although the Association receives adults for their own sake, yet the child is the larger factor in its work.

TABLE III.—ADULTS AND CHILDREN IN 1895.

	Society.	Adults.	Children.	Mixed.	Total.
1	St. J. G.	20,795	36,911	.....	57,706
2	C. A. S.	2,129	9,796	.....	11,925
3	San. H. C.	3,938	10,257	.....	14,195
4	Tribune	.....	6,841[1]	28,924[2]	35,765
5	All Souls'	.....	600	.....	600
6	Barth. Cr.	3,888	7,879	.....	11,767
7	Life	.....	1,180	.....	1,180
8	A. I. C. P.	6,381	13,796	.....	20,177
9	Jr. Rep.	.....	147	.....	147
10	L. M. A.	.....	1,325	.....	1,325
11	S. S. M.	.....	180	.....	180
12	G. A. R. H.	55 (men) 123 (women)	307	.....	485
13	L. a. T. S.	61	219	.....	280
14	C. H. C. H.	.....	2,378	.....	2,378
	Total	37,370	91,816	28,924	158,110

If we suppose the Tribune excursionists to be composed of a somewhat similar proportion of adults and children, or one adult to two children, we have in round numbers 110,000 children who were given outings by these 14 general societies, in 1895. Supposing that some 15,000 of these came from Brooklyn and Jersey City, there remain 95,000 children as New York City's share.

Ages of Child-Visitors.

Although it is impossible to distribute the day excursionists by age classes, data are in hand for ascertaining, at least approximately, the age periods within which fell the 21,820 visitors. Each society has a minimum and maximum age limit for its child-beneficiaries. An occasional exception is made, to admit a child who cannot be left

---
[1] After deducting the 1,180 beneficiaries entertained by Life. 1,662 of the Tribune's visitors were from Brooklyn.
[2] 12,000 of the Tribune's excursionists were from Brooklyn.

at home or who stands in special need of the outing. The classification is sufficiently accurate for practical purposes.

TABLE IV.—AGES OF CHILD-VISITORS IN 1895.

	Society.	1 to 5.	6 to 12.	13 to 17.	Mixed.	Total Children.	Adults
1	St. J. G.	1,043				1,043	600
2	C. A. S.:—						
	Summer Home	....	3,779	....	....	3,779	....
	Health Home	1,776	....	....	....	1,776	1,044
3	San. H. C.	207	567	....	....	774	29
4	Tribune	....	6,841	....	....	6,841	....
5	All Souls'	....	550	50	....	600	....
6	Barth. Cr.	....	....	....	....	....	....
7	Life	....	1,180	....	....	1,180	....
8	A. I. C. P.	....	....	....	325*e*	325	276*e*
9	Jr. Rep.	....	....	147	....	147	....
10	L. M. A.	....	83	....	....	83	....
11	S. S. M.	....	160	20	....	180	....
12	G. A. R. H.	....	....	....	307	307	178
13	L. a. T. S.	....	....	....	219	219	61
14	C. H. C. H.	....	2,378	....	....	2,378	....
	Total	3,026	15,538	217	851	19,632	2,188

It is to be noted that in some cases the age boundaries are somewhat contracted in order to make the age groups intelligently comprehensive. The Little Mother's Aid Association takes girls from 7 to 14; the George Junior Republic, children from 12 to 17; and the Tribune sends a few beneficiaries older than 12, or younger than 6. Instances of such overlapping will partially balance one another in the general summaries. The result of the latter is to show that 90 per cent. of the visitors were children and but 10 per cent. adults. In other words, the adult is much less in evidence in country week work than on the day excursions. The latter are so often made up of young children that the services of the caretaker are in greater demand. The 15 per cent. of children, between 1 and 5, were largely hospital cases. 79 per cent. of the children were from 6 to 12 years of age, or—to be conservative—three-fourths of them.

Expenditures.

What is the cost of their work to the General Fresh Air Societies? As Table V. will show, the fourteen agencies there enumerated have spent more than $1,000,000 upon the charity, not including the cost of plant. Eight of the societies have sanatoriums or "Homes" of their own. The value of their property is as follows.

The basis on which the estimates are made up is indicated in each case:

PERMANENT EQUIPMENT OF NEW YORK'S GENERAL FRESH AIR SOCIETIES.

St. John's Guild:—
    Floating Hospital (official estimate) $25,000.00
    Sea-Side Hospital (official estimate) 45,000.00
Children's Aid Society:—
    Summer Home; construction account to date (1895).. 86,144.10[1]
    Health Home; construction account to date (1895) 52,285.98
Sanitarium for Hebrew Children:—
    Sanitarium at Rockaway Park, L. I. (official estimate) 30,000.00 a
All Souls' P. E. Church:—
    Home at Sea Cliff, L. I.; construction account 26,040.00
Association for Improving the Condition of the Poor:—
    People's Ocean Home, West Coney Island (expert appraisement) 22,000.00
George Junior Republic:—
    Farm at Freeville (official valuation) 4,000.00
Summer Shelter of Morristown:—
    Home in Morristown (official valuation) 4,000.00
Gilbert A. Robertson Home:—
    Land, Building, Live Stock, etc., (Treasurer's report, 1895) 19,208.80
    Permanent Fund 101,387.94
    Total $415,066.82

Property, representing a capital of more than $400,000, is owned by these eight societies.

The data of Table V. have to do with the operating expenses of the charities. If we add to the latter, the value of the permanent equipment, the result will show that more than one and a half million dollars have gone into the Fresh Air enterprises of these fourteen societies. The expenditures in connection with the work of the New York Children's Aid Society, alone, amount to nearly $400,000. Mr. Parsons has disbursed $347,830.29 in sending beneficiaries to the country. No figures are published concerning the expenses of the day excursions managed by the Tribune. Doubtless the total disbursements for both excursionists and visitors would not be far from $400,000. St. John's Guild is a good third in the matter of expense account. These three agencies easily represent an expenditure of a million dollars in connection with the charity. The only enterprise which possesses any considerable

---

[1] Includes cost of property as originally presented to the society.

permanent fund or endowment is the Gilbert A. Robertson Home. Its annual income of about $5,000 is not sufficient, however, to support the work on its present basis.

TABLE V.—EXPENDITURES OF GENERAL FRESH AIR SOCIETIES.

	Society.	Total Expenses (excluding construction.)	Expenses in 1895.	Per Capita.	Per Diem.
1	St. J. G.	$233,855.11[1]			
	Floating Hospital		$16,520.56	$ .29	$ .29
	Sea-Side Hospital		7,552.09	4.59	.56
2	C. A. S.	254,053.60			
	Summer Home		9,253.44	1.00	.37
	Health Home		7,920.65	1.28	.39
3	San. H. C.	65,745.17[2]	9.338.82	.65	.47
4	Tribune	347,830.29	19,840.53	2.47	.17
5	All Souls'	51,773.00	5,566.00	9.27	.69
6	Barth. Cr.	6,810.94	1,183.59	.10	.10
7	Life	48,137.86[3]	3,935.79	3.33	.23
8	A. I. C. P.	55,291.28	10,385.92	.51	.39
9	Jr. Rep.	4,000.00 a	2,508.23	17.06	.28
10	L. M. A.	10,919.89	1,822.00	1.37	1.22
11	S. S. M.	8,742.38	1,576.33	8.75	.62
12	G. A. R. H.	22,662.98	5,539.66	11.42	.94
13	L. a. T. S.	5,000.00 a	1,572.72	5.61	.40
14	C. H. C. H.	15,043.07	8,819.60	3.70	.37
	Total	$1,129,865.57	$113,335.93	$ .71av	$ .30

Perhaps the best idea of the drafts made upon the philanthropy, is to be had from an analysis of the operating expenses for a single year. The expenditures for 1895, exhibit the "standard of living," so to speak, at present maintained by the societies. These expenditures furnish the most reliable basis obtainable for any attempt at a comparative study of the cost of Fresh Air charity in its various forms.

Taking the data for 1895, and dividing the expenses of a given society by the number of its beneficiaries, on the one hand, and by the total days' outings, on the other, we get respectively, the per capita and per diem cost of its work. These items will vary with the individuality of each enterprise. We need above all to know where a society places the emphasis, whether upon excursions or visits to

[1] From 1875.
[2] From 1880.
[3] Expenditures for first three years based on estimates of the number of beneficiaries for those years.

the country. When an organization engages in both forms of the charity, we should be able to separate the expenses of the two. Unfortunately, this is not often possible. One or two societies go so far as to present per capita averages based on a combination of the two types of the philanthropy. The result is an average much too high for the excursionists and too low for the weekly visitors. There are also other things that we need to know before we can intelligently compare the averages given. These have already been touched upon.[1] Reference must be had to the description given concerning the character of each society's work, before the discrepancies between the averages in the several cases can be resolved. The per capita costs range, for example, from 10 cents to $17.06. One represents entertainment for a few hours of a single day; the other maintenance for 60 days of 24 hours each.

A comparison between the per capita expense and the corresponding cost per diem, will show in a crude way the relative amounts of the two types of work in a particular case. Thus where the two items are the same, as with the Bartholdi Crèche, the conclusion is evident—only excursionists are entertained. Where there is a wide difference between the two, the country week type as evidently prevails. The difference in per diem cost between the work of the Floating and Sea-Side Hospitals of St. John's Guild is to be accounted for, probably, by the difference in the length of the day in the two cases, and of the scale on which the two hospitals operate, rather than by any radical differences in methods employed. Again, the two Homes of the Children's Aid Society have almost the same per diem expense, but differ considerably in their per capita expenditure. Yet the length of the visitors' vacations is the same in both cases. How can we account for the discrepancy then? Have we here a reversal of the rule that curative work is more expensive than recreational? The per diem showing would not support the conclusion. The explanation is simple. The larger number of day excursionists received at the Health Home reduces the per capita average at that institution. The largest per diem cost is that entailed by the Little Mothers' Aid Association. The methods employed to find the children, as well as the expense of transportation, account, in part, at least, for the high average. The generous character of the hospitality afforded by the Robertson Home appears from the per diem expense, approaching $1.00 a day. The

---

[1] p. 24.

low average of the Tribune expense, per diem, reveals the part which free entertainment plays in reducing the cost to the Fund. Probably the family-cottage system, as adopted by All Souls' parish, is somewhat responsible for the relatively large expense of 69 cents a day. The analysis might be continued in the case of the other societies, but enough has been said to show the need of knowing the conditions under which each agency operates before trying to establish a hard and fast standard of comparison. The summarized averages of 71 cents per capita and 30 cents per diem are given for what they are worth. By dividing the one by the other the average length of vacation given each beneficiary is confirmed as 2⅓ days.

II.—NEW YORK'S PAROCHIAL FRESH AIR AGENCIES.

We have already touched upon certain limitations imposed on statistical inquiry relating to organizations which address themselves to their own constituencies. To such societies, we have applied the term parochial, as fairly descriptive of their denominational or particularistic character. For the sake of clearness one matter needs further emphasis.

It is with no desire to underestimate the value of the countless agencies coöperating in this work that only societies or churches which conduct Homes for their own constituents are here included. Some such line of demarkation is necessary in order to avoid all sorts of statistical duplications and reduplications. The work of the Charity Organization Society, in its relation to parochial as well as general Fresh Air agencies, illustrates the possibilities of statistical duplication in an inquiry like the present one. For 1895, the society reported 4,939 beneficiaries of Fresh Air relief. 4,371 of these were day excursionists, "paid for by churches and societies," who doubtless recorded these same cases.

The Fresh Air beneficiaries of the New York City Mission and Tract Society are also usually the guests of other summer charities. The statistics of the society for 1895 were:

```
141 day excursionists, making total ........     141 days.
789 visitors, averaging two weeks, making
    total ............... ....................  11,046 days.
         Total .............................    11,187 days.
```

This work cost the society $570.17, or about five cents a day for each person, an impossibly low figure had the society borne the major cost of the outing. We are not, however, to infer that the task of the coöperating Fresh Air agencies, such as the Charity Organization and City Mission societies is a light one. The gathering of a thousand wards means a deal of visitation in the homes of those who are to go to the country or seashore. The candidates for a two weeks' vacation must be cleaned up. Few statistics are available of the number who fail to pass the physician's examination because of over-populated heads.[1] Often, too, the children are to be shod and suitably clothed. Such labor cannot be tabulated, although it is counted an essential part of the charity.

The agencies to be enumerated according to the classification adopted, group themselves in the following way. One parish is omitted, out of deference to the instructions written across the face of the statistics: "Not for publication."

Episcopal Churches	12
Episcopal Sisterhoods	1
Baptist Young People's Union (29 Baptist organizations coöperating)	1
Baptist Churches	1
Presbyterian Churches	1
Ethical Society	1
College Settlement	1
Total	18

The denomination first to take up the work, and the one which has since pursued it most vigorously, is that of the Episcopal church. In New York City, a Fresh Air Home seems now an essential equipment of a well-ordered Episcopal parish. Churches of the denomination, not having Homes of their own, coöperate with sister parishes. For instance, Grace-Emmanuel Church, in 1895, received one-quarter of its income for Fresh Air work from the board of children from other parishes. Nine churches and institutions were represented, the same year, among the guests of the Summer Home of the Church of the Incarnation.

The Baptists furnish an illustration of successful coöperation in Fresh Air philanthropy.

The work of the Methodist Episcopal churches in the city, is

---
[1] See p. 50.

thus described by an official organ of the denomination. "From nearly all our churches bands of 'Fresh Airs' have been sent out by the help of the Tribune, Christian Herald and private funds. Various 'Camps' are in practical operation in which, as principals or partners, we have our share."[1] Methodist Sunday Schools and Boys' Clubs are represented in the citizenship of the Republic of Mr. George, who is a member of the denomination. A "Mothers' Camp," at Westfield, N. J., and a Boys' Camp, in Connecticut, were among the Fresh Air enterprises of the M. E. church in 1895.

A Roman Catholic writer points out the need of his denomination to provide for its own children. "In many instances, far more numerous than we cared to acknowledge, we discovered Catholic children attending Sunday schools of other denominations, where the reward of regular attendance appeared to be a few weeks' outing in the country. Their parents, in many instances, dissipated. . . . The effect on the children may be easily understood. Their young, impressionable minds, finding everything agreeable and pleasant in those country outings, and remembering that everything at home was so different, were led quite naturally to consider their religion as something unattractive. The religion of those with whom they had spent happy weeks was, in their childish eyes, so much nicer than their own because it provided them with pleasanter surroundings." A solution of the difficulty, along the lines of the Tribune's work, had been suggested by Mr. Charles D. Kellogg, of the Charity Organization Society. The result is thus described: "One of the members of the Superior Council (of the Society of St. Vincent de Paul) canvassed different sections of the State of New York. We were all delighted with the success of his mission. Everywhere he was received with open arms, and the result of his visit was that 212 children were provided with homes, each for two weeks, in Catholic families. . . . The Tribune Fresh Air Fund paid the entire expense of their transportation. The Charity Organization Society examined the children; selected those in a condition to go; despatched their agents along with them, and, in addition, brought them safely back to New York. . . . The work must necessarily grow to accomplish what we aim at. Our sole ambition is to preserve for the Church a new generation, thereby adding to her greater glory and advancement."[2] These 212 Catholic children

---

[1] *The Christian City*, August, 1895.
[2] "Outings for Poor Children," *St. Vincent de Paul Quarterly*, Vol. 1., No. 2, February, 1896.

are no doubt included in the Tribune report for 1895, as well as in that of the Charity Organization Society.

Some of the eleemosynary institutions of the city transfer in the summer, certain or all of their inmates to country or seashore. No account is taken of these for reasons given elsewhere.

Remarks on Tables VI. and VII.—It is scarcely necessary to analyze in detail the data of the following tables. They tell their own story of the activity of the religious and special agencies of the city in the exercise of Fresh Air philanthropy. A few things may be noted in passing. The adult is more in evidence in the work of the parochial societies, partly because he is dealt with on his own account. The same is true of the men. St. George's arranges excursions for its Choir, Men's Club and Athletic Club. This church reports a large proportion of the total beneficiaries. Its work, however, being chiefly of the first type does not maintain as large a proportion to the whole when estimated in days' outings. That its 12,019 beneficiaries were not so many distinct individuals appears from its report. "There is no reason why the families should not have been to Rockaway at least three times and the boys and girls of the upper schools five times."

In several instances, we have been obliged to have resort to estimates or partial estimates. In two cases this is made necessary by the classification adopted, whereby inmates transferred from permanent urban institutions to Summer Homes are not counted. In two other instances the information is withheld. In the remaining case, the numbers in one or two of the parties are somewhat indefinite.

The letter *a* indicates where the official returns are furnished approximately. This is usually regarding expenditures. Where estimates are offered, there is more or less official material upon which to base them, so that the results are probably approximately accurate. The additional beneficiaries, "not for publication" may serve as a reserve to make good any inflation in totals.

Because a church has a Summer Home, it does not follow that all of its beneficiaries are entertained there. Grace parish—whose statistics, by the way, are models of completeness—sent its 7,683 excursionists and visitors to twenty different places, but 201 going to Grace House. This fact leads to some slight duplication of records. Grace Church contributed $300 to Mr. George's work in 1895, which amount is included in its own expenditures, although none of its own wards are credited as guests of the Republic.

TABLE VI.—PAROCHIAL SOCIETIES CONDUCTING SUMMER HOMES, 1895.

Society, with Location of Home.	Adults.	Children.	Total.	Excursionists.	Visitors.	Average Days' Stay.	Total Days' Outings.
Baptist Y. P. Union, Somers, N. Y.	...	1,073	1,073	...	1,073	10	10,730
Calvary P. E. Church, Lake Gilead, Carmel, N. Y.	...	...	2,000 M	1,650	350	14	6,550
College Settlement, Katonah, N. Y.	78	78	156	...	{ 126 30 }	{ 12 2 }	1,572
Ethical Society, Thomsonville, N. Y.	...	207	207	...	207	17	3,519
Fifth Ave. Presbyterian Church, Branchport, N. J.	74	468	542	...	542	10	5,420
Grace P. E. Church, Far Rockaway, L. I.	{ 429 m 2,140 w }	5,114	7,683	7,295	388	13½	12,468
Grace-Emmanuel P. E. Church, Sing Sing, N. Y.	...	400 e	400	...	400	14	5,000
Heavenly Rest P. E. Church, Copake, N. Y.	60	456	516	150	366	10¹	3,769
Holy Cross Mission (P. E.), Farmingdale, L. I.	181	309 $p.e$	490	...	{ 480 10 }	{ 14 70 }	7,420
Incarnation P. E. Church, Lake Mohegan, N. Y.	50 e	400 e	450	...	450	7 e	3,150
Judson Memorial Church, Brattleboro, Vt.	{ 10 m 90 w }	489 $p.e$	589	396	193	14	3,098
Sisterhood of Good Shepherd, Asbury Park, N. J.	45 $p.e$	100 $p.e$	145	...	145	10	1,450
St. Agnes P. E. Chapel, Sing Sing, N. Y.	...	116	116	...	116	14	1,624
St. Bartholomew's P. E. Church, Washington and Stepney, Conn.²	...	...	2,227 M	1,940	287	14	5,958
St. George's P. E. Church, Rockaway Park, L. I.	5,409	6,610	12,019	11,459	560	5	14,259
St. Mark's P. E. Church, Morristown, N. J.	...	200	200	...	{ 125 75 }	{ 7 10 }	1,625
St. Thomas' P. E. Chuch, East Marion, L. I.	30	363	393	...	393	15+	6,020
Trinity P. E. Church, Islip, L. I.	27	454	481	...	481	14	6,734
Total	8,623	16,837	29,687	22,890	6,797		100,966

a Approximate.   *p.e* Partly estimated.   *m* Men.
e Estimated.   *M* Mixed.   *w* Women.
¹ Nearly. Total days allotted visitors, 3,619.   ² Two boarding places controlled by the management.

TABLE VII.—EXPENDITURES OF PAROCHIAL SOCIETIES, 1895.

Society.	Expenditures, 1895.	Per Capita.	Per Diem.
Baptist Y. P. Union	$2,504.00	$2.33	$ .23
Calvary P. E. Church	2,500.00 a	1.25 a	.38 a
College Settlement	1,018.52	6.52	.04
Ethical Society	2,600.89	12.56	.73
Fifth Avenue Pres. Church	3,140.91	5.79	.57
Grace P. E. Church	3,492.25	.45	.28
Grace-Emmanuel P. E. Church	1,919.82	4.79 p.c	.34 p.c
Heavenly Rest P. E. Church	2,001.69	3.87	.53
Holy Cross Mission (P. E.)	1,818.26 p.c	3.71 p.c	.24 p.c
Incarnation P. E. Church	1,553.70 p.c	3.45 p.c	.49 p.c
Judson Memorial (Bap. Church)	1,000.00 a	1.69 a	.32 a
Sisterhood of the Good Shepherd	475.00 p.c	3.27 p.c	.32 p.c
St. Agnes Chapel (P. E.)	435.67	3.75	.26
St. Bartholomew's P. E. Church	2,820.20	1.26	.47
St. George's P. E. Church	3,049.58	.17 exc'sts.	.17
		1.77 visitors.	.35
St. Mark's P. E. Church	1,500.00 a	7.50 a	.92 a
St. Thomas' P. E. Church	2,218.04	5.64	.36
Trinity P. E. Church	3,809.71	7.92	.56
Total	$37,858.24		

On the basis of Tables VI. and VII., we may sum up the work of these 18 parochial societies as follows: 29,687 beneficiaries, including 6,797 visitors, received 100,966 days of outing at an expenditure of $37,858.24.

III.—*WORKING GIRLS' VACATION SOCIETIES.*

The Working Girls' Vacation Societies represent a distinct variety of Fresh Air charity. What differentiates them from the common type is the fact that the beneficiary contributes, as a rule, to the expense of the outing. These agencies are therefore, to that extent, philanthropic rather than charitable. Since, however, the payments of the beneficiaries are sufficient to meet but a minor part of the expense attendant on the enterprise, such Vacation Societies may properly be included in a study of Fresh Air Charity.

The Working Girls' Vacation Society.—This society sprang from a desire to provide summer outings for girls older than the maximum age limit allowed by the Tribune Fresh Air Fund. The success of the initial efforts of Miss Katherine Drummond—now Mrs. Herbert—the president of the society, to supplement the Tribune's work, led to the formation of a society distinctly for working girls. This was in 1884. The philanthropy has always been of a non-sectarian character.

For the first few years, the society relied for entertainment upon carefully selected country boarding places. More recently, two or three Summer Homes have been presented to the organization. These accommodate a considerable number of the girls. It has been found necessary to restrict the benevolence of the society to such as are broken down in health. A physician's certificate is required in every case. Two reasons are given for this. "In the first place, the society has become so well known among working girls that in a fortnight enough applications would be received to exhaust all our money, were we to say that we would send away those in good health. Then we also feel that in helping such as are ill, worn out or convalescent, we are in no way pauperizing the girls." Besides providing places of entertainment for working girls, the society also furnishes transportation to such as have friends whom they might visit in the country. More than 10 per cent of its beneficiaries have come under this head.

We take no account here of the distribution of Glen Island tickets furnished the society at a reduction to be sold to working women, nor of the aid rendered in supplying them with addresses of reliable and reasonable boarding places. Many of the beneficiaries are cash and stock girls from the department stores, their wages ranging from $2.50 to $3.00 a week. About a fourth of them are from Brooklyn and neighboring cities. The society has been aided in the raising of funds by the Christian Union, now called the Outlook, which collected $12,646.03 for the philanthropy from 1891 to 1895, inclusive. In the decadence which at present seems to mark the once popular and profitable "Fair" as a source of revenue, this alliance with a well-known weekly journal is a fortunate one.

The Jewish Working Girls' Vacation Society.—The society was incorporated in 1892. According to the constitution, "the objects of this society are to assist worthy Jewish working girls of small means to spend their summer vacation at a country home to be provided for them where the Jewish dietary laws and observances shall be kept, and where they may rest and recuperate." To this end, the society rents a Summer Home to which its beneficiaries are sent. The girls who are able, pay $3.00 a week for their board. As a rule all pay their own car fare.

Those whom the society particularly wishes to help are "the girls who live in the crowded East-side and down-town districts, overworked and under-fed, and who, though sick and suffering, cannot cease from the work which, too often, means the only support of an entire family."

The Vacation Farm Society.—The society began its work in 1893 by leasing a Summer Home or "Vacation Farm." Its aims and methods are not dissimilar from those of the Working Girls' Vacation Society. In fact, at its annual meeting in December, 1895, the Vacation Farm Society decided to work thereafter in coöperation with the senior organization.

TABLE VIII.—WORKING GIRLS' VACATION SOCIETIES.

Society.	Date.	Beneficiaries.	Average Days' Stay.	Total Days' Outings.	Total Expenditures.
Working Girls' Vacation Society	1884	6,886	14	114,863	$81,528.32
		879	21		
Jewish Working Girls' Vacation Society	1892	396[1]	10e	3,960	3,289.89[1]
The Vacation Farm Society	1893	227 a	14	3,178	3,386.71
Total		8,388		122,001	$88,204.92

STATISTICS FOR 1895.

	Beneficiaries	Average Days' Stay.	Total Days' Outings.	Expenses.
Working Girls' V. S.	640	14	11,018	$11,209.00
	98	21		
Jewish Working Girls' V. S.	80	14	1,505	1,692.06
	55	7		
Vacation Farm Society	79	14	1,106	971.18
Total	952		13,629	$13,872.24

RECEIVED FROM BENEFICIARIES.

	Total Amt. so Received.	Percentage of Expense.	Receipts in 1895.	Percentage of Expense.
Working Girls' V. S.	$15,823.84 p.e	19.4 p.e	971.80	8.6
Jewish Working Girls' V. S.	1,395.20[2]	42.4	600.30	35.4
Vacation Farm Society	994.58	29.3	330.00	33.9
Total	$18,213.62		$1,902.10	

Remarks on the Statistics.—The one feature which calls for

---

[1] Statistics for 1892 are wanting.
[2] No financial statement at hand for years previous to 1894.

special notice is that which differentiates the working girls' vacation societies from the ordinary Fresh Air charity, namely: repayments by beneficiaries. What stress, as a matter of fact, is laid upon this principle in the practical operation of the philanthropy? So far as the smaller societies are concerned, the revenue from this source in 1895 was about a third of the expenditures. In the case of the largest and oldest of the working girls' societies the showing is not so favorable. Since 1884, the repayments have amounted to about 1-5 of the expenses. In 1895, they were less than 1-10. Moreover, the following percentages show that the decline has been more or less constant for a series of years.

    1890 Percentage of Repayments to Expenditures 28.2 per cent.
    1893 Percentage of Repayments to Expenditures 17.4 per cent.
    1894 Percentage of Repayments to Expenditures 11.4 per cent.
    1895 Percentage of Repayments to Expenditures 8.6 per cent.

The years given are the only ones in which the society has distinguished between receipts from the sale of Glen Island tickets and repayments from beneficiaries sent to the country to board. It is with the latter only that we are concerned. Questions of some importance arise in this connection. Is the senior society among the vacation agencies for working girls on the road to becoming a purely charitable institution, thus losing the distinctive feature of "self-help?" What causes have operated to bring about such a decline in repayments? (1) Does the society now minister to a class of girls less able than former beneficiaries to bear a portion of the cost of the outing? (2) Or does the same class receive a smaller wage owing to hard times, for example, and less constancy of employment? (3) Is there any change in the policy of the society itself? (4) Is any relation traceable between increased resources and greater generosity?

Statistics can answer these queries but in part. The following analysis is offered for what it is worth:

Year.	New Features.	Expense[1] Per Capita.	Cost of Board.	Repayments.
1884	Girls, if able, pay $1.25 a week....	$8.17	$7.96	$243.00
1885		7.80	7.50	881.76
1886	Presented with Green's Farms	7.93	7.35	1,692.42
1887	Girls pay $1.50 a week	8.42	7.71	2,365.98

[1] Railroad tickets and traveling expenses of beneficiaries are not included. Of course, no account is taken of those sent to friends in the country. Their expense to the society is chiefly a matter of transportation.

Year.	New Features.	Expense Per Capita.	Cost of Board.	Repayments.
1888	Physician's certificate required	9.28	8.32	1,551.87
1889		10.02	8.84	1,574.78
1890		....[1]	8.31	1,689.58[2]
1891	"Christian Union" coöperates	9.83	8.76	2,288.70
1892	Opening of "Cherry Vale"	11.74	9.39	2,138.37
1893		12.49	9.20	1,528.61[2]
1894	House at Craigville opened and furnished	12.68	8.12	1,184.87[2]
1895	Opening of Santa Clara cottage ... Opening of Elmcote cottage[3]	14.72	7.50	971.80[2]

Certain things are noticeable from this analysis. One of these is that the cost of board has remained practically stationary, being the same in 1895 as in 1885. On the other hand, the expense per capita shows increase, particularly at two stages of the enterprise. The moment the philanthropy decided to confine its attention to the girl broken in health, the cost per capita increased. Hospital treatment, as we have seen before, means enhanced expense. The repayments, so far as we can judge from the financial statement of the society, do not seem at once to have decreased on this account. The second period marked by a decided increase of expenditure, came with the definite change of policy made possible by an increase in resources. The report for 1892, says: "We have too often found that, in spite of all contracts, the food has been poor or insufficient, while the farmer's wife had so many duties in the kitchen that she had no time to give to the girls themselves. For this reason we are happy over the offer of a gift of a piece of property less than two hours from New York.

"Our idea is to make this the nucleus of a little settlement, or park. After a while we hope that others may feel disposed to give us cottages, in which case we can enlarge the main house (which the society was to build) to meet the requirements." While this plan has not been carried

---

[1] The data required for a per capita estimate in 1890, are not separable from railroad tickets and other items.

[2] Repayments given for these years are exclusively from "Visitors." For the other years receipts for sale of Glen Island tickets are included. The latter may be roughly estimated as a third of the total amount.

[3] "Elmcote" took the place of the cottage at Craigville. About $1,400 were spent in furnishing the two houses, which largely accounts for the increase per capita over 1894.

The Outlook makes it one of the conditions of its coöperation with the Working Girls' Vacation Society that the matrons shall be hired by the year. "The Outlook's Vacation Fund," *The Outlook*, Vol. 54, No. 24, December 12, 1896, p. 1,077.

out, as yet, the society has more and more made the "Summer Home," rather than the farmer's family the place of entertainment. This change of policy is marked by a decided increase of incidental expenses, using the term to cover everything but the item of board. In the meantime, not only have repayments diminished relatively but they have increased absolutely. The report for 1895 states that "Each girl is required to pay the nominal sum of $1.50 per week, excepting in cases where the person recommending the applicant assures us that she is not able to do so." How often the latter must have been the case appears from the fact that, judging from the total repayments, not more than one-half paid this nominal board. The conclusion, to which we are led, would seem to be that all four of the causes above cited (p. 81) have a share in bringing about the decline of repayments. Causes (3) and (4) are probably the most potent.

GENERAL SUMMARY OF FRESH AIR WORK IN NEW YORK CITY.

```
Number of General Fresh Air Societies reported ...... 14
Number of Parochial Fresh Air Societies reported .... 18
Number of Working Girls' Vacation Societies reported  3
                                                     ___
      Total ........................................  35
```

The 14 General Societies report their total Fresh Air work as:
```
Day excursionists ............................ 1,225,278
Visitors (average 10.9 days) .................   257.583
Days' outings ................................ 4,037,642
Value of property ............................ $415,066.82
Expenditures (exclusive of construction) ....$1,129,865.57
```

STATISTICS FOR 1895.

	General Societies.	Parochial Societies.	Working Girls' Vacation Societies.	Total.
Adults	37,370	8,623	952	46,945
Children	91,816	16,837	...	108,653
Mixed	28,924	4,227	...	33,151
Total	158,110	29,687	952	188,749
Excursionists	136,290	22,890	...	159,180
Visitors	21,820[1]	6,797[2]	952[3]	29,569[4]
Days' Outings	367,792	100,966	13,629	482,387
Expenditures	$113,335.93	$37,858.24	$13,872.24	$165,066.41

[1] Average visit, 10.6 days.
[2] Average visit, 11.4 days.
[3] Average visit, 14.3 days.
[4] General average, 10.9 days.

CHAPTER IV.

DISCUSSION OF GENERAL PROBLEMS.

In addition to the request for statistical data, the present inquiry invited certain general information, and also suggestions touching possible improvements in the practical operation of Fresh Air charity. The points covered by the circular letter were:

1. The various forms of entertainment employed by the philanthropy.
2. Methods of selecting beneficiaries.
3. To what extent, if any, beneficiaries contributed to the cost of the outing.
4. What means were taken to prevent duplication.
5. What evidence there was of a tendency on the part of the beneficiaries to look to the Fresh Air agencies for assistance in other directions.
6. How far the charity was proving itself an educational force.
7. Personal recommendations and suggestions for the perfecting of the work.
8. Actual results of Fresh Air endeavor.

It is now in order to discuss these topics in the light of our statistics and of the official replies to the general inquiries to learn what conclusions may be drawn from the experience of the societies themselves. In this way we may hope to arrive at some theories of Fresh Air work which shall be at once inductions based upon the actual operation of the charity, and conclusions derived from the application of scientific principles of relief work in general.

The Various Forms of Fresh Air Relief.

The topic covers questions 7 and 9 of the letter of inquiry. The subject, being so closely related to the statistical part of the present study, has been treated already from that standpoint. We have seen that Fresh Air agencies are of two kinds, the excursion type and the vacation or country week type. While the beneficiaries of the excursion societies are largely in the majority, the total days' outings are not always in their favor. It remains to sum up certain relative advantages and limitations of the respective types.

Day Excursions.—The day excursions possess certain qualities which are sufficiently advantageous to account for their wide-spread popularity. In the first place, they accommodate those who cannot remain from home overnight. For mothers who cannot be spared from their families, and infants and young children who may not be separated from their mothers, this is the only form of summer outing available.

Again, such outings allow a certain amount of flexibility. Those in special need of recuperation can be taken on a series of excursions. While care is necessary to guard against the presence of infectious diseases, more laxity is permissible in the matter of dress and cleanliness of person than is the case with the candidates for country week. The bath is frequently an important function of the day's outing. Thus, the very poor, without regard to nationality or creed, are eligible to such excursions. A third advantage of great weight undoubtedly in the minds of the projectors is the small pro rata cost of the outing. Called upon, as a rule, to furnish neither breakfast, supper, nor lodging, the day trips are comparatively inexpensive. Frequently excursionists provide their own luncheons. Attendants are relatively few. The operation of the charity by "wholesale" reduces expenses to a minimum. House to house visitation in selecting the beneficiaries may render the day excursion the most expensive form of Fresh Air relief. The per capita expenditures of 7.2 cents and $1.22 respectively represent the two extremes of cost, as well as of method.

Experienced Fresh Air workers have testified in the course of the inquiry, to the advantage which day excursions have, in that the family may be treated as a unit. At least the mother and her younger children are eligible to the privileges of such outings.

On the other hand, two limitations in the excursion type of Fresh Air relief stand out prominently. Both have found ample illustration in certain very recent exhibitions of the day excursion in New York City, where false sentimentality backed by inordinate ambition for newspaper circulation seems to have been the prevailing motive.[1] The first of these limitations is the

---

[1] One of the worst features connected with the excursions in question, in the summer of 1896, was the means employed to secure contributions for the charity. The streets were patrolled by young girls who solicited money in the name of the "Fund." The effect upon the children was such that the Society for the Prevention of Cruelty to Children felt constrained to interfere in order to protect these girls from being trained in the ways of pauperism and immorality. (See article entitled "Babies' Fund Beggars," The Evening Post, New York, Tuesday, July 28, 1896.) The writer had occasion to watch the effect of this sort of alms-seeking in the case of two girls about twelve and fourteen years of age, who accosted him on successive days, soon abandoning the pre-

liability that these outings will assume the character of free-for-all picnics. This danger is reduced in proportion as physical ailment as well as poverty is made the condition of relief. Wherever tickets may be had for the asking the danger is imminent. A second drawback is the loss of individuality. Frequently the size and promiscuous gathering of the parties render this result inevitable. Routine and a certain military precision are essential to order. One cannot see the individual for the crowd. This need not necessarily detract from the physical benefits of the outing, though it must needs promise less satisfactory moral returns. Doubtless the majority of the beneficiaries are so accustomed to live and move with the multitude, that they themselves do not so much object to this feature. Some societies, particularly parochial ones, meet the difficulty by restricting the membership of the party to certain related groups or by furnishing families with tickets to neighboring picnic resorts.

Country Week.—In contrasting the two types of Fresh Air charity, the advantages of the one form of relief are, in a sense, the limitations of the other. It is the longer vacation, for example, that affords opportunity for intellectual and moral betterment, as well as physical improvement. The quiet influence of family life and the personal relation of the child to its caretaker have time to make themselves felt. Either directly or incidentally, a certain amount of instruction in the art of living is practicable. We found that where an approximate age classification was possible, as in the case of the general societies of New York City, 70 per cent. of the country week visitors, in 1895, were children between the ages of 6 and 12. This is the period at which the child may be separated temporarily from its parents, often to the advantage of both. It is the impressionable age, when the child is keenly alive to the stimuli of a new environment. In the country week type of the charity, greater discrimination is the rule in the selection of beneficiaries. The fact that so much more is to be given, in this case, makes it the more necessary to guard the privilege from abuse. Where a society engages in both forms of the philanthropy, the neediest are the ones who

tense of offering in return various trinkets exposed for sale. When a passer-by ventured to challenge their authority, the ready response was: "Why, didn't you see my picture in the paper?"
With the introduction of electric street railways and the reduction of fares to seaside and country resorts, the necessity of furnishing free transportation is correspondingly curtailed. From New York City one may now go to Coney Island and return for fifteen cents, or from Brooklyn for ten cents.

come in for the enjoyment of a visit to the sanatorium or the Home.[1] Thus the cumulative benefits of the longer vacation are shared by those who will profit most by them.

After all has been said as to their relative merits, one must conclude that the day excursion is to country week, what the occasional day's outing of the business man or tired housewife is to the ordinary fortnight's vacation in the summer. Each has its own place. Where the second is not possible, the first is all the more essential. But for permanent benefit, nothing can take the place of a complete change of scene for a succession of days.

The Family, and the Summer Home or Colony.—Where shall those who go as visitors be sent? As a matter of fact we have seen that the family is less in evidence than the Home. Moreover, where the visitor is inducted into the former, he goes more frequently as a boarder than as a guest. The emergencies of the case would seem to be sufficient to account for this fact. Nothing can be so economical for the societies as voluntary entertainment. Yet the difficulty of securing free hospitality, year after year, for an increasing number of wards is so considerable that most of the larger Fresh Air agencies have come to depend either upon boarding places or Summer Homes. An expert in relief work offers a valid objection to bringing the invited guest and the boarder to the same locality. Where the two systems are brought into competition, the springs of private hospitality are dried up. Charitably disposed country folk will hardly be willing to sacrifice their own comfort and convenience by receiving children of the tenements as their guests, while their neighbors, equally well-to-do, find the Fresh Air boarder a source of income. The effect of such a competition calls for the practice of mutual comity on the part of societies whose methods of hospitality thus conflict.

The payment of board offers this much of advantage, that a certain selection and supervision are possible which must seem impertinences in the case of free entertainment. The testimony of country week societies which board their beneficiaries in farm houses is the same as that of agencies which "place out" dependent children, namely, that "accommodation can be found for many more children than the number sent."

---

[1] Such, at least, is the theory. It is to be feared, however, that the right which certain patrons of charitable societies claim, to name the beneficiaries of the funds contributed by them, makes the exception not uncommon. It takes real heroism for a charitable society to refuse the "requests" of wealthy supporters.

The real question, however, is not so much between forms of family entertainment as it is between the family and the summer colony. The statistics of the general societies, not including vacation societies for working girls, show 13 instances where Fresh Air agencies rely upon the family and 35 societies which send beneficiaries to Summer Homes. At the conference of Fresh Air workers in 1888, this resolution was adopted as the sense of the meeting: "That the placing of children in individual homes, either as boarders or invited guests, is the policy best adapted for the formation of habits of thrift and self-respect, and of ambitions for physical, mental, and spiritual improvement, because it brings the children into such close contact with the refining influences of virtuous homes." "Why does not the Country Week establish houses of its own with matrons in charge?"—is the question frequently put to the Boston society. After twenty-one years of experience, the answer is: "Because we have learned from experience and observation that the present methods are more economical and better adapted to the welfare of our beneficiaries. We want *homes* for them, not *institutions.*"

This is directly in line with the teachings of scientific charity with regard to the care of dependent children.[1] It is interesting to note that New York City, which is so wedded to the public institution in the care of its dependent and delinquent children, most fully illustrates at the same time the idea of colonization in Fresh Air relief. Do the evils of the one system inhere in the other? Or how far may we argue from the one to the other? An analysis of the actual situation will probably be enough to show that we may not justly impute to the average Fresh Air Home the evils of eleemosynary institutionalism.

Two facts are sufficient to differentiate the summer colonist from the ward of the public institution. In the first place, the children, as a rule, come from families that are respectable, although poor. The beneficiaries have the training that comes from such homes. Then again, two weeks is scarcely long enough to "institutionalize" anybody.

As to the relative merits of entertainment in the private family and the Summer Home, we have the testimony of two Fresh Air

---

[1] See New York State Charities Aid Association's pamphlet, No. 59, "Proceedings of a Conference on the Care of Dependent and Delinquent Children." Also pamphlet No. 63. See too "Massachusetts' Care of Dependent and Delinquent Children," published by Massachusetts Board of Managers, World's Fair, 1893.

workers in a large colony. Their own families had previously been in the habit of receiving Fresh Air children into their homes. Both strongly favored the plan of colonization. They were sure that more could be done for the visitors and that they had a better time in the larger Home.[1]

One can readily understand that the city child whose playground is the street, has few resources for its own entertainment when taken to the country. In the one case, everything depends upon the disposition and leisure of the hosts. On the other hand, where a colony provides itself with a sufficient number of caretakers, particularly if they are trained kindergartners used to children and their needs, one may believe that it is quite possible to individualize the beneficiaries effectually. Where, in addition, the cottage system is employed to break up the colony into family groups, the advantages of both methods may be secured. The serious objection to the latter system is the additional expense involved.

Undoubtedly the maintenance of small homes, either widely separated or grouped in a single settlement, entails increased incidental charges. Yet there is reason to believe that the economical possibilities of the cottage system have not been exploited. To this end the houses should be simple yet convenient and homelike in their appointments; the food nutritious and abundant; everything scrupulously neat; and bathing facilities ample. On the other hand, all luxuries should be eschewed. For it may well be questioned whether we do a kindness even to the "daughters of the tenement" when we introduce them to standards of living which can only serve to emphasize with exquisite cruelty the barrenness of many of their own homes.[2] Furthermore, any approach to luxury which should tempt a society to select Fresh Air candidates who will fit its Home rather than to suit the Home to the candidate, is to be regretted. Wherever it appears that entertainment in Summer Homes entails

---

[1] Compare these arguments for the summer colony: Children are more difficult to manage in private families; the teacher is a better moral authority than the family; the food is worse where the child is boarded out. In the settlement, the children have a livelier, happier time; and teachers and scholars in their friendly intercourse become better acquainted. Such are the arguments of Pastor Bion, the founder of the "Ferienkolonien," or Vacation Colonies, of Switzerland. See the Charity Organization Review, Vol. IV., p. 346.

[2] The remark of a warm friend of the working girl comes to mind in this connection. "There is altogether too much *coddling* of the working girl," said she, as we were talking of Fresh Air work. How generally this is true only those may judge, who, like the speaker, are devoting their lives to their sisters' cause.

an expense nearly double that involved by sending to carefully selected boarding places in the country, this fact alone constitutes an argument against the former plan. With the *à priori* conclusion, based upon the methods of relief work in general, decidedly in favor of the boarding out system, with the practical results obtained by country week societies demonstrating its value, the burden of proof rests upon the advocate of the Home. Certainly it may fairly be doubted whether the advantage of the latter warrants any considerable increase of per capita cost, particularly in view of the fact that, other things being equal, as expenses increase the number of beneficiaries must decrease.

While the effort is making to avoid extravagance and luxury, the institutional spirit needs shunning as well. The latter tendency is easily fostered wherever societies erect great Fresh Air establishments accommodating hundreds of children. The large colony is to be kept full even if the demand for Fresh Air has to be created.[1] "We cannot do justice to any more," was the sentiment expressed to the writer by an expert superintendent of a Fresh Air Home caring for more than four hundred city wards. Surely the danger line of institutionalism has been reached when a single management must be responsible for so many beneficiaries.

No special mention has been made of the parochial Home where the selection of visitors is from a distinct constituency. Here is a chance for the element of personality to enter to a degree that is scarcely possible where the relationship established is but for a few days or weeks.

Methods Used to Select Beneficiaries.

The degree of relationship between a society and its wards is indicated in some measure by the way in which the latter are selected. In reply to the question: "How are the children selected;

---

[1] Are there other supporters of the charity in New York City whose experience tallies with that of a worker who had been sending children to the country for twenty years? Opportunities had multiplied, till now, she said, "It is hard to get children enough." This had led to unseemly competition among those who gather up the children.

The warrant for the multiplication of Fresh Air societies has been the contrary assumption that there is a *dearth* of opportunities for summer outings among poor children. Much of the strength of the argument against sending the same children to the country more than once in a season, is in the assumption that there is a "waiting list" of worthy candidates. If the latter is not the case, a halt should be called to the increase of general Fresh Air societies, and the enlargement of the present Fresh Air plants.

by your own visitor; through other societies; or otherwise?" the answers group themselves as follows:

13 Societies outside of New York City, select their beneficiaries by means of their own visitors, or in an equivalent manner.
6 Agencies select their wards through other societies.
11 Societies employ sometimes one method and sometimes the other.

The methods in vogue among the general societies of New York City are described elsewhere. The parochial associations, working with their own clientage, naturally employ the more personal and direct method of selection. In short, this matter depends almost entirely upon the nature of each particular Fresh Air society.

Contributions of Beneficiaries.

20 Fresh Air societies, not including those of New York City, receive nothing from beneficiaries. 9 such societies receive "something" "sometimes," ranging from "luncheons" to possibly one-third the cost of the outing. Not more than two of the associations appear to have a settled policy to develop self-help by means of money payments. One out of ten of the beneficiaries of the Working Girls' Vacation Society of Brooklyn pays something, while the City Missionary Society of New Haven reports that beneficiaries are "allowed and expected to do so if able."

Of the general societies of New York City, the beneficiaries of the Bartholdi Crèche pay their own car fare. In 1895, some of the visitors to the George Junior Republic did the same. The adults received by the Lana ac Tela Society either pay for themselves or are paid for by their own friends. The treasurer's report for 1895, shows that 20 per cent. of total expenses was returned in money for board. There is nothing to show what part of this was directly contributed by adult visitors. The president estimates "roughly" that one-half the women pay for themselves. This is the only one of the 14 general societies reported that received any repayments for entertainment in 1895.

8 of the 18 parochial societies encourage beneficiaries to share the expense, at least of fares. In two instances, the amounts contributed did not exceed 3 or 4 per cent. of the total cost, while in two other cases they rose to 17 and 20 per cent. respectively. The College Settlement Society has a sliding scale of charges for its visitors. They pay in the aggregate about 1-5 of the expenses. "Older ones pay $3.00; middle-sized ones, $1.50; children, $1.00."

With the working girls' vacation societies, we have seen that repayments are the rule, to which there are many exceptions.

From this survey of the field one is warranted in concluding that repayments for *children* are rare and usually insignificant.

The Fresh Air Conference of 1888, so often referred to, resolved: "That partial payments, whenever possible, by the parents, in the cases of children boarded or colonized, in the form of either stated sums per week or of car fares, is wise, and to be recommended by this Conference as inculcating independence and thrift, and discouraging the neglect of parental duties."

An English authority on Fresh Air work, commenting on the discussions of the Conference, thus contrasts the English and American methods in this matter: "The greatest difference between the two methods is to be found in the amount of responsibility left to parents. In America 'no attempt is made, as a rule, to exact payments from the parents.' In London the proportion of the whole expenses of the Children's Country Holidays Fund borne by the parents in 1888 was 32 per cent."[1] In 1893, the parents contributed 37 per cent. of the income of the society.[2] One of the district committees of the association "estimates the actual cost of the child at home, independently of rent and other permanent charges and requires the parents to contribute this amount, unless there are any special reasons for remission." Another committee reports that parents in a majority of cases are anxious to contribute toward the expense to the very utmost of their ability.[3]

One society, which makes it a rule to send away no children whose parents are earning more than 30 shillings a week, received, in 1893, 23 per cent. of its income from the parents of its beneficiaries.[4]

Is there any reason to suppose that the American is less able than the English workingman to share the expense of his children's country holiday? Why then, should he not be encouraged to do so? "Transform it all into cheap boarding-houses on the sliding scale. Better to pay something, if it is only 25 cents—it would certainly cost that much to keep the children at home." Such is the advice of the rector of a mission church in New York City, advice which he puts into practice in his own successful Fresh Air work.

[1] Cyril Jackson, in Charity Organization Review, Vol. V., pp. 169, 170.
[2] Charities Register and Digest, 1895, p. 223.
[3] Charity Organization Review, Vol. VII., p. 359.
[4] "North St. Pancras Children's Holiday Fund," Charities Register and Digest, 1895, p. 223.

How far would such a policy be practicable in the case of the general Fresh Air societies—say of New York? The present system of free hospitality is thoroughly intrenched. It appeals to the generous impulses of contributors. Then, too, the societies themselves value that sense of independence that comes from receiving their wards as free visitors rather than partial boarders. Were parents to share their children's vacation expenses, criticisms on the managements—the one thing now gratuitously contributed by beneficiaries—would doubtless multiply. Were a single organization to initiate the reform, it would manifestly be at a disadvantage in filling its Homes. Were several societies to act independently of one another in fixing rates of charge, the experience of English Fresh Air workers would probably repeat itself in the way of "unhealthy *competition* for the custom of the poor."[1]

The fact that the Charity Organization Society of New York City reports partial repayments from but 1 per cent. of its nearly 5,000 Fresh Air beneficiaries in 1895, shows the prevalence of the free system—the more clearly as the society works through a large number of churches and other agencies. It will surely be a cause for regret if the example of free hospitality shall prove so contagious as to lead any one of the working girls' vacation societies to abandon the principle of self-help which now differentiates them from the other Fresh Air charities. We may venture to express the hope that any decline in the amount of such contributions is but temporary, and that the management will cherish the early policy, even at the loss of individual patrons who may be tempted to use their contributions as claims upon a society's free bounty. We may yet hope to see a wider extension of efforts to help those who are ready to help themselves, and the insistence upon a larger parental responsibility in the matter of partial payments wherever these are possible in behalf of children. However, before there can be a general adoption of a system of repayments in cities like New York and Boston where there are numerous Fresh Air agencies in the field, greater coöperation among the societies than now exists will be essential to success.

Means to Prevent Duplication.

Information on this point from 25 general Fresh Air societies

---

[1] "Country Holiday Work in Central London," Charity Organization Review, Vol. XII., No. 142, Nov., 1896.

outside of New York City may be summarized in the following way:

    10 Societies take measures to prevent duplication.
    2 Societies make some attempt in this direction.
    2 Societies answer in the negative.
    6 Societies reply that they are the only Fresh Air agencies in their respective communities.
    5 Societies offer general remarks.

The methods employed to prevent duplication vary in completeness and effectiveness. This appears from attempts to classify the answers given. Here are samples: "Registration. None sent twice the same year unless very sick." "General inquiries are made." "We investigate each case." "All are investigated and records kept." "We only send those we know and see often." "Nothing definite, except our own lists; no great danger of too much being done." "Names, addresses and ages are recorded." "Asking for lists of names from other societies of those sent." Two agencies, the Country Week, of Boston, and the Charity Organization Society, of Baltimore, are known to have made recent attempts to bring the Fresh Air workers of their respective cities into coöperation. The secretary of the Baltimore society writes: "With regard to registration: the three Homes have registered with us all summer (1896), mailing lists to our Central Office, which were immediately indexed and returned, with all duplications marked. The expense has been very slight—we did not find it necessary to employ an extra clerk because our work is less heavy in summer time, and the small expense of postage and stationery we were glad to bear ourselves. . . . . . . The three homes failed to show any great amount of duplication, although we discovered some at the beginning. I think the mere fact of sending lists to us, and of having it known by those who prepared the lists, that they were to be sent, made them more careful." The success of the experiment was handicapped by the failure of the largest Fresh Air society of the city to coöperate with the others in the registration.

What is the situation in New York City? Societies employ such methods of recording beneficiaries as they deem sufficient for their own work. Careful inquiry has failed to discover any systematic conference or coöperation between the societies to guard against "repeaters" or duplication of one another's efforts. The recommendations of the Conferences of 1888 and 1891 have been duly received and placed on file. Here the matter rests. In the general absence of alphabetical lists of beneficiaries, it is impossible to prove by a comparison of such lists how far Fresh Air repeating is practised in the city. There is no reason to suppose that with the multiplication of Fresh Air societies the danger has decreased since attention was first called to it. Nor is it to be presumed that this form of relief is an exception to others in its liability to abuse corresponding to its lavishness. The table that is herewith presented will exhibit some of the possibilities of the situation.

Society.	Age Limits.	Condition.	How Selected.	Means to prevent Duplication.
St. J. G.	Young Children and Mothers	Sick or Ailing	Dispensaries, Societies, etc.	None employed
C. A. S. Health Home	Young Children and Mothers	Sick or Ailing	Dispensaries, Societies, etc.	None employed
Summer Home	7-14	Need	C. A. S. Schools, Missions	None employed
San. H. C.	Children, 1-9, and caretakers.	Need	Adults apply at downtown office	None employed
Tribune	6-12	Need	Workers among the poor	Reliance upon those selecting
Tribune Excur's	Children and Mothers	Need	Workers among the poor	Reliance upon those selecting
All Souls'	6-12	Need	Visitor, etc.	Visitor's knowledge and care
Barth. Cr.	Children and Mothers	Ailing	C. O. S., Dispensaries, etc.	"None required. Only children liable to illness received."
Life	(See Tribune)			
A. I. C. P.	All ages	Need	Own Visitors	Visitation and registration
Jr. Republic	12-17	Need	Missions and Personally	Children taken for July and August
L. M. A. A.	7-14	Need	Chaperons	Investigation
S. S. M.	6-12	Need	Through N. Y. Societies	None (by S. S. M.)
G. A. R. H.	Families	Need	Application Bureau	"Close investigation."
L a. T. S.	All ages	Need	Personally, Churches, etc.	Request no duplicates be sent; question wards
C. H. C. H.	6-12	Need	Pastors and Superintendents	An alphabetical list of beneficiaries

In the light of the above table let us examine the Fresh Air

[1] In a brief synopsis like this it is impossible to draw any but broad lines of demarkation. Sickness and Need are relative terms. Physical necessity is the prime essential for relief in the one case, material necessity in the other. The Junior Republic deals also with cases of moral destitution.

opportunities of one placed under certain conditions. Take a woman with four children, the youngest an infant in arms, and the oldest a "little mother" twelve years of age. There is a girl of four and a boy of seven. All except the baby are among the thousands of children that attend the schools of the Children's Aid Society. They are also members of a mission Sunday school. The mother is glad to secure free board for herself and children for as many weeks in summer as possible. She, thanks to the baby, who is a bit ailing, is eligible to the Health Home, and the other three children are invited to spend a week at the Summer Home of the Children's Aid Society. The older children have already been promised by their mission teacher that they should go to the country when vacation time came.

Besides the Homes provided by the churches, there is the Christian Herald Children's Home, which is noted for its hospitality, and a trip to the country through the Tribune or Life Fund is not out of the question, especially should the children belong to a mission, or the clubs of one of the social settlements. If the baby chances to be seized while at home with acute bowel trouble, there is the sanatorium of St. John's Guild, or, if the case is less serious, the excursions of the Floating Hospital are available. Probably it would be difficult to secure a fortnight for the entire family at the Robertson Home, unless arrangements had been consummated before the other outings were matters of history. Failing this, there is the Association for Improving the Condition of the Poor, whose visitor to the family the previous season perchance made the winter of their discontent glorious summer, by anticipating with them the privileges of the "Ocean Parties," followed by a visit to the Ocean Home. The time has come for pledges of hospitality to be redeemed.

Such a happy combination of circumstances as is here supposed would be comparatively rare, though others almost equally promising might be substituted.

One of the most experienced administrators of both general and Fresh Air charity in the city testifies to conversations frequently overheard between adult beneficiaries, in which comparisons of various Fresh Air Homes were made, accompanied by boasts of the number visited in a single season. A matron of a Summer Home illustrates her own experience with this class of "rounders" by the story of a woman in vigorous correspondence with other Fresh Air societies while a guest of the first.

Interviews with the children in summer colonies would probably discover that their opportunities for summer outings are not as limited on the whole as sometimes fancied. Such at least is the writer's impression from a few talks with those who confessed to other vacations either prospective or retrospective.

The secretary of a Fresh Air society in New York says of the work in general: "We are imposed upon, of course, tremendously so," and of duplication in particular, he adds: "We can't check it." The president of another society writes: "I wish something could be done to prevent children and adults from going away more than once, thereby preventing many others from having an outing at all. We feel sure this has seldom happened at the ——— Home, but we also feel sure it *must* happen frequently in larger homes where less personal attention is given by those in charge."

Although the parochial societies have better means of knowing their beneficiaries than have the general agencies, the former cannot be sure under present methods that their wards do not avail themselves of the general societies' bounty. By belonging to different missions, Fresh Air, like Christmas, privileges may readily be multiplied. The means taken to prevent such duplication are: "Watchfulness." "We do not usually take those who have other outings." "Children only received that attend Sunday school or day nursery." "Personal knowledge of the families." "Only persons known to us are sent." "No objection to sending twice when change is needed." "Do not receive Sunday school children who attend other schools."

If it should still be asked what are the real objections to duplication, there are three that may be mentioned briefly. (1) The moral effect upon the beneficiaries. Deliberate repeating is sure here, as in other forms of relief, to demoralize sooner or later those who indulge in it.

(2) Wastefulness. The expense of Fresh Air work where itinerancy exists is proportionately increased. Duplicate transportation, registration and attendant costs of administration are involved.

(3) Inequality in the distribution of Fresh Air privileges. This is the most serious of the objections. The most importunate seekers for Fresh Air relief are seldom the most worthy. Such is the testimony of those best acquainted with the charity, and tallies with experience in other forms of relief distribution. The supposition that New York City's provision of Fresh Air privileges is sufficient for all who are in actual need of such assistance is based on the assumption that the charity is fairly distributed.

A canvass of 200 families made last December under the direction of Mrs. Fullerton, Superintendent of Relief of the N. Y. A. I. C. P., disclosed the following facts. It should be said that the families selected were those known to have received excursion tickets from the A. I. C. P. during the summer of 1896.

Members of 105 families went 1 time, receiving 105 total days' excursions.
"   " 46   "   "   2 times, "   92 "   "   "
"   " 14   "   "   3   "   "   42 "   "   "
"   " 7   "   "   4   "   "   28 "   "   "
"   " 8   "   "   5   "   "   40 "   "   "
"   " 6   "   "   6   "   "   36 "   "   "
"   " 14   "   " 8-40 "   " 200 "   "   "
      ───   ───
"   "200   "   "   543 "   "   "

Average of 2.7 days' excursions per family.

Besides the day excursions, members of 23 of these 200 families received a vacation of a week or fortnight at a Summer Home. A total of 28 weeks or 196 days was thus distributed. Adding these to the excursion outings, we have a total of 739 days, or an average of 3.6 days to each family. The misleading character of such an average appears from the fact, that, according to the above figures, members of 14 families received 200 of the total days' excursions; that is, 7 per cent. of the families received 36 per cent. of the single day's outings.

Actually, 225 families were visited, but 25 of them had moved since the summer, which fact marks the shifting of this class of the population and is to be reckoned with in any attempt to follow up the work of the summer by friendly visitation in the winter.

The most marked cases of duplication or of successive excursions were these:

Case 1:— With N. Y. A. I. C. P. .... 1 excursion.
         With Evening World .... 15 excursions.
         With Children's Aid Society .. 1 week at the Home.

Case 2:— With N. Y. A. I. C. P. .... 5 excursions.
         With Evening World .... 2 excursions each week during season.
         With Children's Aid Society .. 1 week at its Home.
         With Children's Aid Society (Brooklyn) 1 week at its Home.

Case 3:— With N. Y. A. I. C. P. .... 2 excursions.
         With Evening World .... 2 excursions per week in season.
         With St. John's Guild .... 2 excursions per week in season.

Case 4:— With St. John's Guild .... 5 excursions a week for the season.

It is to be remembered that these reports are based on the testimony of the persons receiving the outings. While the families interviewed would have reason to conceal the truth, they had no reason to exaggerate the facts.

In conclusion, one can but regret that the data for ascertaining, even approximately, the amount of overlapping and "overlooking," that actually exists in New York City, for example, are so incomplete.

Has Fresh Air Charity any Tendency to Pauperize Its Recipients?

One way in which such a tendency might be expected to show itself is indicated in the question: "Is there any tendency on the part of the recipients to come upon the society for assistance in other directions, *apparently as a result of this work?*" Of 29 Fresh Air agencies outside of New York City that reply to the question, 23 societies find no such tendency, while 5 organizations do find such a tendency, "occasionally," "in many instances," "in very few cases," "for clothing slightly," or "much aid given unsought." One society expresses doubt about the matter.

Of the general societies of New York City, but two may be said to reply in the affirmative. Dr. Tolman answers: "Yes, I believe so." Mr. George writes: "There was until this season " (i. e., 1895, when the Camp was organized as a Children's Republic to meet this and other difficulties). Mr. George tells the story of an Italian child who was forever assailing him during the vacation with the stereotyped question: "What yer's goin' ter give us when we go home?" Finally, in desperation, the answer came, "I don't know that I will give you anything." The girl's eyes flashed fire as she retorted: "Well, what yer's tink we's here fer, anyway?" His experience with similar cases convinced him that many of the children were sent for the sake of the "spoils" which they were expected to bring away with them.

None of the parochial societies appears to have discovered the tendency in question.

It is but fair to note certain characteristics of Fresh Air work which operate to check any pauperizing tendency inherent in general charity. One of these self-operating checks is found in the fact that so many of the societies are not general relief agencies. Our statistics have shown that 29 out of 51 societies are distinctively Fresh Air associations. Whatever relief is afforded is directly connected with this charity. Doubtless, as Mr. George points out, this does not entirely free the charity from opportunities to pauperize. The intermittent character of the work is a second check. The charity is a summer philanthropy. Its temporary nature breaks the continuity of the relief afforded. It may encourage a kind of amateur pauperism, but is not sufficiently permanent to satisfy the demands of professionalism. The professional, however, may make use of the charity to secure free board in season.

We have previously noted the bearing which the matter of age has upon the question. So far as young children are the recipients of the relief, only the parents are affected in this respect by the moral influences of the charity. As we have seen, however, the majority of vacation visitors are children between the ages of six and twelve. Such beneficiaries, like Mr. George's Italian ward, are old enough to appreciate the advantages of getting something for nothing. Illness, too, is usually considered a condition which invites the minimum danger of pauperizing recipients of relief. Hospital treatment has an important place in Fresh Air ministrations. Restrictions in the way of standards of cleanliness will operate as checks. Whatever calls for effort on the part of the parents or entails sacrifice will have a similar effect. Some mothers are found who are too lazy to prepare themselves or their children even for the day excursions. Where it is necessary to cut off the hair of the child, the parental pride is often too great to pay the price more than once.

If in addition to such checks as already exist, there were introduced the system of partial repayments, together with a central registration bureau to guard against repeating, any tendency to pauperize beneficiaries would be reduced to a mimimum. If, moreover, it shall be found that the charity exerts a considerable educational influence on its recipients, a further guarantee that its distribution is safe-guarded will be afforded.

Fresh Air Charity as an Educational Force.

This does not necessarily imply the giving of formal instruction. The Conference of 1888 discouraged attempts in this direction, "inasmuch as the influences for good that spring up spontaneously in a pure home can be safely left to their unaided work." On the other hand, one of the arguments in behalf of the summer colony is that "the teacher is a better moral authority than the family." This may mean simply that the teacher is a better disciplinarian. Certainly, if definite instruction is recognized as one of the aims of the outing, this is a strong point in favor of the colony, where trained teachers may be employed.

The kind and amount of instruction at present afforded, exhibit considerable variety. Yet that the vacation is valued for the lessons which it conveys appears from the replies of a number of societies.

14 Agencies answer that no instruction is attempted by them.
11 Agencies answer in the affirmative.
3 Agencies reply that instruction is given incidentally.

When one inquires as to the nature of the instruction imparted, one finds that it ranges from "preaching on Sunday" to "systematic kindergarten teaching." The replies also include, "Sewing, housework and kindergarten teaching." "Books for reading." "All incidental instruction that can be given is given." "It is hoped that habits of neatness, order and industry will be taught the visitors" (this from a society that boards out its beneficiaries). "Children are instructed a few hours every day." "Only that of kind suggestion as to more thrifty ways of living, cooking, etc." "Instructive games are provided."

It may be of interest to compare with the foregoing, answers from the general societies of New York city. "No; children go for a good time." "Gratitude and the Golden Rule." "Personal talks to women and children by trained nurse and kindergartner." "Instruction is given in various trades, in citizenship, government, social life, etc. It is a miniature Republic of the children, for the children, and by the children." "Instruction in morals and manners." "Instruction in dish-washing, bed-making, waiting on table, mending, manners, correct language, etc." "Housework, sewing." A station of the Penny Provident Fund is maintained on the Floating Hospital of St. John's Guild. Here also mothers are instructed as to the bathing and care of their children. This last is true of other sanatoriums.

The parochial societies respond: "Religious training, housework, sewing, some school-work." "Service morning and evening. Singing and library—Sabbath afternoon services." "Yes, two or three hours a day by teachers from the Workingman's School, Instruction in Botany, Zoology, Landscaping, etc." "Education in housework. Informal teaching about plant and animal life." "No; children go for Fresh Air."

There appear to be but two or three instances where the instruction can be considered formal in its nature. The Junior Republic is one of these. The work here is directly educational, endeavoring to develop moral energy and purpose in the vacationists while acquainting them with the elements of republican institutions. A visit of two months makes systematic instruction practicable. The Society for Ethical Culture provides science teachers for its beneficiaries. The children are from its city school and have the advantage of previous training in similar lines of work. The summer outing affords opportunity for field work in nature studies. Attention has already been directed to the efforts of the N. Y. A. I. C. P. to combine recreation and education.[1] The lessons here are more or less informal, but good results are reported in the teaching of the arts of marketing, cooking and the like. Kindergarten instruction and nature work are also provided.

Whatever invites intellectual effort on the part of recipients of Fresh Air charity, or tends to store within them moral as well as physical energy, will in so far free the philanthropy from any suspicion of pauperizing its beneficiaries. That it is possible to develop the educational purpose at the expense of the recreational is quite conceivable. Re-creation is the motive of Fresh Air work. Physical recreation should work itself out in improved disposition and habits when the child returns home, and in renewed power of application at school.[2]

Perfecting Fresh Air Charity.

One naturally looks to the societies themselves to point out any deficiencies which at present exist in the charity and to indicate how these may be supplied. Therefore it will be well to give at length the replies to the question: "How can the work be improved?"

---

[1] P. 56. On this point see 53d Annual Report of the Association.

[2] As appears from the answers to the general inquiry, many of the churches and missionary societies value the work for the opportunity which it furnishes for imparting religious teaching. Ecclesiastical agencies should studiously avoid all appearance of using their Fresh Air hospitality as a vehicle for proselyting to their own communions. Such suspicion is more naturally occasioned where children are received not only from the Sunday school, but as members of secular clubs and classes connected with the parish.

For example, here is a description of a work to which a devout Romanist might take exception. "A few of the happy faces have been seen in our Sunday school, but the majority of this group are Catholics, attending our Boys' Club." So much for the character of the Fresh Air party. This is the program of the camp life. "It is decided to rise early, bathe, take breakfast, then hold service. . . . We decided to have a little Gospel meeting each evening under different leaders. . . . Almost from the first, at the services, texts were given out to be learned by heart, chapter and verse; prizes were offered, and the competition was very earnest."

SUMMARY.

	Generally Applicable.	Specific Answers.	Satisfied at present.
Replies of Societies outside of N. Y. City..	5	6	2
General Societies of New York City	5	1	2
Parochial Societies of the City	4		

One society considers the subject too large to enter upon, and two others think their experience too recent to warrant advice from them. Answers are considered "specific" which relate to the affairs of the particular society, usually, as it happens, with reference to increased resources.

The president of the Allegheny City society suggests improvements:

(a) "By having more thorough visiting among the poorer classes."
(b) "By having some school instruction for the children."
(c) "By having some training for the mothers, as to the care of their children; also instruction in sewing."

Remarks:—"I should like to see some *industrial* training for the children, that, in addition to their health, they might carry back some other valuable helps for a better living. I would like to see regular teachers employed for a part of every day, and a training class for the mothers as to a better, happier, healthier way of caring for their children."

This is from one of the Baltimore societies:

(a) "By beneficiaries paying a nominal sum."
(b) "If many of the families could be followed up during the winter by a friendly visitor, a much more permanent effect would be secured, and many of the parents, whose confidence has been gained by the kindness shown the children, could be influenced in many ways for the better."

The agent of the Lake Geneva Fresh Air Association writes:

"I advise thorough investigation, full coöperation with others engaged in the same work, that the real merits of each case may be known. A registration of names and addresses, that others engaged in the same work may have access to. The general rules observed by relief societies concerning applications, visitations and decision of cases might be observed in this work with advantage. In our own work we give preference to invalids (not hospital cases), to convalescents, or cripples, and a decided preference to those who have not been sent to us before."

The secretary of the Hartford City Missionary Society emphasizes these things:

(a) "Persuade public and private parties to register the names of children sent, through a Charity Organization Society or some central place."

(b) "Careful selection of children."
(c) "Careful selection of families receiving them."
(d) "Careful instruction of both families and children beforehand."

Remarks:—"There should be a central place where each child should be prepared with a bath and general cleaning up just before starting. The families who entertain should understand these children get their ideas of good home-life, of cleanliness and order, of kindness and love and Christian living during their visit, and these are more helpful in promoting their best good than any physical benefit received and will be more lasting. If such good homes could be found it would be better than boarding together in a public home."

The secretary of the Worcester City Missionary Society recommends:

(a) "Great care in selecting those who are worthy."
(b) "Systematizing to the last degree."
(c) "Following up the families aided through the year."

The suggestions from those interested in the Fresh Air charities of New York seem to relate more or less directly to the societies of that city.

The president of All Souls' Summer Home writes:

"Coöperation is always desirable and there should be a meeting of Fresh Air workers once every spring."

The general agent of the N. Y. A. I. C. P. recommends:

(a) "Some kind of Fresh Air Clearing House."
(b) "Less regard for proselyting by the churches."
(c) "More loving coöperation by the philanthropies."
(d) "A higher standard in the individual work."

Mr. George speaks of things taught him by his own experience and suggests reforms which he has instituted at his summer camp:

(a) "By taking occasion during their outing to teach them the rudiments of some useful trade.
(b) "By devising some systematic method of payment for the work they perform at the above mentioned trade, amount received governed by quality of work. Payment need not necessarily be in United States currency. Little cardboard checks will serve the purpose just as well."
(c) "By requiring payment for board, lodging, clothing, and, in fact, everything they receive, with the money or the checks mentioned in 'b'."

The city manager of the Gilbert A. Robertson Home says:

(a) "Avoid crowding your homes."

(b) "Take time in forming your parties and endeavor to have them congenial."

The president of the Lana ac Tela Society writes:

(a) "I think homes should be located nearer the city, so more could be taken and less expended on car fare."

(b) "By personal work on the part of those in charge, not trusting oversight and management to paid attendants, who, in many cases, have no love for the work."

(c) "By small homes and more of them where individuality is not swallowed up in the large number received."

(d) "By combining instruction with the pleasure of the outing and in all cases emphasizing the idea that some return must always be made for the good things we receive if we are to have self-respect."

The few suggestions offered by the parochial societies are in brief:

(a) "By providing moderate boarding places for working girls and young men who do not wish to be under the charge of any Charitable Association."

(b) "By providing more places where whole families may be taken together."

(c) "By conducting work on plan of partial repayments, provided exception is made in extreme cases."

(d) "More small cottages would aid greatly in keeping the work from becoming an aggregation."

(e) "By extending its scope."

(f) "Extension of day excursions to avoid breaking up the family."

The recommendations may be summed up—somewhat after the order of the prominence given them—as: More friendly visitation, instruction, partial repayments, central registration, general co-operation between Fresh Air societies, more personality in the work, careful selection of beneficiaries and hosts, application of general rules of charitable relief, less proselyting by churches, thorough systematization, more small homes, avoidance of overcrowding, homes nearer the city, more provision for families as a whole, and for working girls and young men who do not wish to be objects of charity, but are willing to pay moderate board.

Does It Pay?

On one point the societies are practically unanimous, and that is that Fresh Air work pays. The emphasis in the affirmative is unmistakable from such expressions as: "Most certainly it does pay." "Surely it does." "Over and over again." "We know of nothing that pays better." The 28 societies outside of New York that reply to the query, answer in the affirmative. A few give specifications. "Improvement in health and cleanliness. Suggestions of better habits of living. Knowledge of country life." "By reducing mortality among the infants of the city." "In every way, particularly by giving an open door of access for religious effort to the home benefited." "Physically; yes."

In New York City the endorsement of the charity is quite as cordial. "Beyond a question." "Certainly it does." Mr. George, alone, qualifies his answer. He thinks that the charity needs to be on its guard, "Otherwise—to be perfectly frank—I believe there are instances where children are pauperized through the securing of 'something for nothing.' Make the good old maxim, 'Nothing without labor,' a law with the children and it will pay abundantly."

The parochial societies agree with the more general agencies, that the work is highly remunerative.

Our American societies have made few, if any, scientific tests to ascertain the exact physical improvement in Fresh Air beneficiaries. One physician of considerable experience with the general results concludes that very poor children are not as much benefited as the better class, "because (1) they are in a state of chronic hunger; (2) the time is not long enough to make much of an improvement, and (3) the slight benefit they derive is not permanent, because they return to the same mode of life." Dr. Daniel continues: "I have sent children for six or seven years, but have not definite statistics, yet my impression is that at least one-half of the children sent are improved physically. The most marked improvement is in appetite and general appearance. I can say that I believe the Fresh Air Fund is the best plaster we have for unjust social conditions of the people."[1]

The physical benefits derived from the Vacation Colonies of Switzerland have been made the subject of careful analysis. An examination of 34 children showed an improvement in blood coloring of 18 and 26 per cent. for the boys and girls respectively, and in blood corpuscles of 25 and 32 per cent., a condition well maintained four months after their return from the Colonies.[2]

[1] Letter to Rev. Willard Parsons, and quoted by Mr. Parsons in "The Story of the Fresh Air Fund," Scribner's Magazine, Vol. IX., No. 4, April, 1891.
[2] "Sanitäre Erfolge der Zürcher Feriencolonien im Jahre 1895." Dr. Leuch, Stadtarzt in Zürich. Dr. Leuch concludes the report of his investigation with these words: "Gestützt auf solche Erfahrungen stehe ich als Arzt und Hygieniker keinen Augenblick an, die Feriencolonien als

Having thus reviewed the information obtained in response to the letter of inquiry, it only remains to summarize the results and conclusions of the study.

In Chapter I., the purpose of the present paper is indicated and its general limits are defined.

In Chapter II., the work of thirty-seven general Fresh Air societies—not including similar agencies in New York City—is discussed from the standpoint of statistics, and definite data respecting the distribution, development, volume, range, types, cost and methods of the charity are presented.

Chapter III., is a detailed study of the Fresh Air activities of a single city. New York, because of its relation to the charity at its inception and the rapid multiplication of Fresh Air agencies there, has offered a promising field for closer investigation.

In the present chapter, we have discussed in the light of the statistical data and of general experience, certain specific problems relating to the practical operation of the philanthropy.

We are now prepared to answer the questions raised at the beginning of the inquiry. The conclusions to be drawn have been already more or less definitely anticipated in the course of the discussion. They may therefore be the more briefly summarized here.

The justification of Fresh Air charity rests upon the assumption that its beneficiaries are physically and materially in need, and therefore unable to secure for themselves or their children those curative and recreational opportunities vouchsafed to their more fortunate fellows, and essential to the maintenance of normal vigor or the successful pursuit of daily tasks.

Whatever rules are applicable to the distribution of general relief are also applicable to the distribution of Fresh Air relief. Promiscuous alms-giving stands condemned. Experience proves that society may have as many dependents as she is willing to provide

---

eine der segensreichsten sanitären Institutionen zu bezeichnen, deren unzweifelhafte Erfolge um so höher angeschlagen werden müssen, als sie nicht blos vorübergehender, sondern dauernder Natur sind und nicht blos den betreffenden Kindern, sondern durch diese auch der Gesammtheit zu Gute kommen."

M. Guyau, in his noted work, "Education et herédité," warmly endorses "les colonies de vacances et les voyages de vacances." He quotes the words of his countryman, M. Cottinet, experienced in the philanthropy, to show its hygienic value. "Et l'on a pu constater ces deux choses d'une éloquence égale; avant leur départ pour la campagne, le poids de ces enfants, la circonférence de leur poitrine, sont fort au-dessous, lamentablement au-dessous de la moyenne assignée à leur âge; à leur retour, la proportion s'est renversée: ils ont gagné de cinq à dix, à vingt fois l'accroissement normal." (Education et herédité." p. 112.)

for. The distinction between sentimental charity and scientific relief is not one of motive but one of vision. Difference of vision leads to difference of method. Both the sentimentalist and the sociologist desire to satisfy need. The one, however, is conscious only of the individual and the present moment. The other sees society in the individual and takes counsel of the future. Scientific charity seeks therefore to discriminate between the worthy and the unworthy, and to restore those who are dependent through no fault of their own, to a place of self-respect in the economic world. While, as we have seen, Fresh Air relief commonly possesses certain checks which reduce the danger of pauperizing its beneficiaries, this fact does not absolve the charity from due care in the distribution of its favors.

If then we accept the fact that Fresh Air work as here classified is a charity, and as such is to be governed by the rules of organized relief, much is gained for its scientific administration.

How shall the ailing and the needy be sifted from the mass of importunates except by some kind of test, registration or investigation? And how may the worthy poor who shrink from asking charity in any form and who have no friends to speak for them, be discovered except by some plan of visitation? With an annual distribution of some half-million days' outings and the expenditure of more than $150,000 in the case of a single city like New York, must all attempts to coördinate the work of the several Fresh Air societies be abandoned? Dr. William I. Hull, in charge of the Department of Sociology and Economics at Swarthmore College, after a summer's practical experience with the workings of Fresh Air charity in New York, sums up the situation as follows:

"The task of criticism is always an unpleasant one, and in the name of charity many sins should be forgiven; but there are certain evils which cannot be forgotten, and which every effort should be made to avoid. Our experience in the Bureau of Invitations has led us to the conclusion that a great deal of summer charity covers at least two great evils, namely, ignorance of the true status of those sought to be benefited and consequent injury to them and others; and, secondly, an overlapping in the work of charitable agencies. As an instance of the first, when it was ascertained that a family recommended to us for a fortnight's stay at the Homes was in receipt of sufficient income to enable them to occupy rooms with a monthly rental of $40, the no doubt well-meaning individual who recommended them replied, when asked for an explanation of why she had recommended them: 'Oh, I am only a missionary, and you cannot expect me to know such things.' Again, when leading newspapers and charitable societies march beneath the

DISCUSSION OF GENERAL PROBLEMS. 109

banner of 'Philanthropy, Notoriety and a Long Subscription List,' they are often led to reap in a field already harvested, and an injurious reduplication of Fresh Air Charity ensues. This, we regret to say, has been the case in our city during the past summer. It is not contended, of course, that everyone who needed an outing received it. The pity of it is that the 'old rounders' who know all about the charitable agencies and pursue them diligently through summer and winter, and who often stand in least need of such outings, receive most of them; while thousands of the city's poor and invalid, not knowing of these opportunities of securing rest and strength, or not caring to enter into an unseemly pursuit of them, receive them not."[1]

Here is expert testimony. If now the plan tried this last summer in Baltimore and already described seems too complicated for New York's manifold Fresh Air agencies, why should not an experiment similar to the one suggested by the Conference of 1891 be fairly tested? One season's trial would demonstrate the wisdom or otherwise of further coöperation. Let each society agree to keep an alphabetical list or card catalogue of the names of its beneficiaries with the number of days' outings given to each during the summer. At the end of the season, let such lists be submitted to the Charity Organization Society for inspection. Let the lists be compared and all cases of duplication *between societies* be carefully noted, together with the number of total days' outings enjoyed by such beneficiaries. Let these cases be visited and their actual physical and material condition be ascertained. If it should then appear that the overlapping has been very considerable and that it has occurred largely in the case of the less worthy to the exclusion of the more deserving, let a conference be called and some form of practical coöperation be devised for the following season. Several advantages would accrue from such an endeavor. (1) It would furnish an object lesson in organized coöperative charitable effort. (2) It would call for a systematic registration of beneficiaries on the part of *all* the Fresh Air societies. (3) The experiment would demonstrate how far the charity is at present subject to abuse. (4) Finally, if serious duplication were discovered, doubtless some practical method would be devised to prevent its continuance.

Such efforts at coördination might ultimately lead to the forma-

[1] A. I. C. P. Notes, Vol. I., Nos. 4 and 5, p. 64. Dr. Hull notes the fact that of the families applying or recommended to the N. Y. A. I. C. P.'s Fresh Air Bureau, 23 per cent. were rejected for various reasons, "the most common ones being that their financial condition did not justify gratuitous aid, that their physical condition did not require Fresh Air Charity, or that they had already been the recipients of Summer Outings."

tion of a Central Council composed of representatives of the various Fresh Air Societies,[1] and the division of the tenement section into districts with a system of regular visitation by experienced workers for the purpose of ascertaining the needs and resources of the several wards and of furnishing relief to children and their elders somewhat in the order of the necessity.

All this may be but an idle dream. One may well wish, however, that a charity which rallies to its support all sorts and conditions of folk—the artisan and the clerk, the child and its parents, the devotee of the club and the woman of society, the secularist and the churchman, the democrat and the Sultan of Turkey—might set that example of practical coöperation for whose consummation scientific charity waits. In the meantime, let all efforts municipal and private, which aim to bring Fresh Air privileges or their equiva-

---

[1] For the sake of record, it may be noted that the "Conference of Charities of the City of New York," at its monthly meeting, April 21, 1897, held in the United Charities Building, considered the topic: "Fresh Air and Summer Charities." The writer, by request, submitted to the Conference a plan for a Central Council of the Fresh Air Societies of the city. The plan was discussed by the Chairman of the meeting, Rev. Willard Parsons, and by the following invited speakers: Hon. John P. Faure, of St. John's Guild; Dr. H. E. Crampton, of the Association for Improving the Condition of the Poor; Mr. Nathan Lewis, of the Sanitarium for Hebrew Children; Mrs. J. H. Johnston, of the Little Mothers' Aid Association; Mr. Charles Loring Brace, of the Children's Aid Society, and Mr. James E. Dougherty, of the Society of St. Vincent de Paul. Other speakers were Mr. Homer Folks, Secretary of the Conference, Dr. Moreau Morris, and Rev. John B. Devins. The following resolutions were presented and passed without a dissenting voice:

RESOLVED, That a Committee of Five, consisting of the Chairman of this meeting, the principal speaker of the meeting, the Secretary of the Conference of Charities and two persons to be appointed by the Chairman, be appointed as a Committee to take the initial steps in behalf of the Conference of Charities, in the formation of a Council of Fresh Air and Summer Charities in New York City, and

RESOLVED, That the duties of this Committee shall be as follows:

1. To fix a time and place for the first meeting of such a Council.

2. To issue invitations in the name of the Conference of Charities to each of the general societies engaged in Fresh Air and Summer Charity, inviting them to send a delegate to the proposed Council of Fresh Air and Summer Charities.

3. To ascertain whether any of the societies in this building will furnish office room for a clerk of the Council of Fresh Air and Summer Charities during the summer months without charge.

4. To formulate an estimate of the expense involved in carrying on the work of the Council during the summer months in accordance with the plans outlined at this meeting.

5. To formulate and present to the first meeting of the Council a plan of organization.

6. To take such other preliminary action as may seem to them necessary in arranging for the first meeting of the Council.

lents within the reach of the everyday life of the people, be quickened and multiplied. These efforts relate to improved housing, small parks and children's playgrounds in the tenement sections, a system of dock parks where practicable, training classes for mothers, vacation schools, baths and lavatories, and the development of rapid and cheap transit facilities lessening the breach between country and city.

Far better than any charity even at its best is the distribution of such social and economic opportunities as will make wholesome normal living possible for the denizens of the tenement and their children.

BIBLIOGRAPHICAL AND OTHER SOURCES OF MATERIAL.

Annual Reports of the Various Fresh Air Societies.
Answers to the Letter of Inquiry issued in the name of the N. Y. A. I. C. P.
Correspondence with Officials and Workers connected with the Charity.
Interviews with such Officials and Workers in New York, Brooklyn, Boston and elsewhere.
Visits to Fresh Air Homes and Colonies, and attendance on Excursions.
Year Books of Churches, and Denominational Publications.

SPECIAL ARTICLES IN CURRENT LITERATURE.

"An Ideal for the Children's Country Holidays Fund."—Charity Organization Review (London), Vol. X., No. 116; September, 1894.
Barthélemy, Antonin, "Country Holidays for Paris Children."—C. O. Review, Vol. II., No. 24; December, 1886.
"Children's Country Holidays in Berlin."—C. O. Review, Vol. III., No. 25; January, 1887.
Cole, William I., "Country Week."—New England Magazine, Vol. XIV., No. 5; July, 1896.
Germain, Eugene, "Vacation Colonies in Switzerland."—Consular Reports, Vol. LII., No. 193; October, 1896.
Gilman, M. R. F., "Our Country Weekers."—Lend a Hand, Vol. II., No. 10, October, 1887.
Hull, William I., Report to General Agent of N. Y. A. I. C. P.—A. I. C. P. Notes, Vol. I., Nos. 4 and 5; December, 1896.
Humphrey, E. F. (Miss), "Country Holiday Work in Central London," Charity Organization Review, Vol. XII., No. 142; November, 1896.
Jackson, Cyril, "The Children's Country Holidays Fund," Charity Organization Review, Vol. V., No. 52; April, 1889.
Lovett, Eleanor I., "One Summer's Work."—Sunday Afternoon, Vol. I., No. 5; May, 1878.
"Outings for Poor Children."—St. Vincent de Paul Quarterly, Vol. I., No. 2; February, 1896.
"Outlook's Vacation Fund (The)."—The Outlook, Vol. LIV., No. 24; December 12, 1896.

Parsons, Willard, "The Story of the Fresh Air Fund."—Scribner's Magazine, Vol. IX., No. 4; April, 1891.
Perkins, J. Newton (Rev.), "The First Summer Home and its Founder."—The Churchman, Vol. LXXIV., No. 11; September 12, 1896.
Rideing, William H., "The Charities of a Summer."—Sunday Afternoon, Vol. III., No. 21; September, 1879.
Times, New York, Files for the Summer Seasons, 1872-1875.
Wiley, William H., "A Glance at the Guild's Early History."— Monthly Bulletin of St. John's Guild, Vol. IV., No. 7; November, 1895.

FOREIGN REPORTS.

Bericht über die am 8. u. 9. August, 1896, in Berlin abgehaltene Fünfte Konferenz der Vertreter von Vereinigungen für Sommerpflege. Berlin, 1896.
Bericht über die Ergebnisse der Sommerpflege in Deutschland im Jahre 1892. Berlin, 1893. Similar reports for 1893-1895.
XVII. Rechenschaftsbericht des Berliner Vereins für häusliche Gesundheitspflege. Berlin, 1896.
Die Ferienkolonien für arme Schulkinder in der Schweiz in den Jahren 1891-1895, zugleich Überblick über die ersten 20 Jahre der Entwicklung: 1876-1895. Von Harald Marthaler, Bern, 1897.
Ferienversorgung in Basel. Berichte und Rechnungen, 1878-1892. Basel, 1894. Also reports for 1895, 1896.
Zum XXjährigen Bestand der Ferienkolonien. Erstehung und Entwicklung derselben. Bericht von Zürich, 1895, von W. Bion, Pfarrer. Zürich, 1896. Similar reports, 1883-1894.
Sanitäre Erfolge der Zürcher Feriencolonien im Jahre 1895. Von Dr. Leuch, Stadtarzt in Zürich. (Separatabdruck aus dem Correspondenz-Blatt für Schweizer Aerzte, 1896, Nr. 21.)

GENERAL BIBLIOGRAPHY.

Charities Review, The; New York, 1891—
Charity Organization Review, The; London, 1885—
Charities Register and Digest, London, 1895.
Hand-Book of Sociological References for New York. By Wm. Howe Tolman and Wm. I. Hull; New York, 1894.
Life and Work of William Augustus Muhlenberg, D. D. By Anne Ayres; New York, 1880.

New York Charities Directory; New York, 1895 and 1897.
Proceedings of the National Conference of Charities and Correction; Chicago, 1893. (See index for articles on the Care of Dependent Children and Child-Saving.)
Publications of the State Charities Aid Association; New York. (Especially Nos. 59 and 63.)
Report of Health Department, City of New York, 1892. Memoranda of the Department, Dr. Roger Tracy; New York, November, 1896.
Report of the Tenement-House Committee of 1894. Albany, New York, 1895.
Slums of Great Cities, The; Seventh Special Report of the Commissioner of Labor, Washington, 1894.

www.ingramcontent.com/pod-product-compliance
Lightning Source LLC
Chambersburg PA
CBHW031350160426
43196CB00007B/800